SOUND DESIGN AND MIXING IN REASON

quick **PRO**
guides

Sound Design and Mixing in Reason

Andrew Eisele

HAL•LEONARD®

An Imprint of Hal Leonard Corporation

Published in 2012 by Hal Leonard Books
An Imprint of Hal Leonard Corporation
7777 West Bluemound Road
Milwaukee, WI 53213

Trade Book Division Editorial Offices
33 Plymouth St., Montclair, NJ 07042

Printed in United States of America

Book design by Adam Fulrath
Book composition by Kristina Rolander

Library of Congress Cataloging-in-Publication Data
Eisele, Andrew.
  Sound design and mixing in Reason / Andrew Eisele.
     p. cm.
  Includes index.
1. Reason (Computer file) 2. Software synthesizers. 3. Software samplers. 4. Software sequencers. I. Title.
  ML74.4.R43E38 2012
  781.3'4536--dc23
                              2011047989

ISBN 978-1-4584-0229-5

www.halleonardbooks.com

CONTENTS

Chapter 2

Chapter 3

Chapter 4

Chapter 5

Chapter 1

SOUND DESIGN AND THE SYNTHESIZER

What Is a Synthesizer?

A synthesizer is an electronic device that generates waveforms. There are a number of different types of synthesizers (e.g., video synthesizers, voice synthesizers, audio synthesizers). In this chapter, we'll be focusing specifically on synthesizers used for audio applications.

The advent of the synthesizer, and its subsequent popularity in the late 1960s and throughout the '70s, changed forever the landscape of music and sound design. The concept of imitative synthesis, whereby a device is used to emulate a particular acoustic instrument, has been a huge boon for the advancement of the technology of synthesis. For instance, if you want to add the sound of a violin or oboe to a musical piece, but neither play said instrument nor have the ability to hire someone who can, a synthesizer would prove an invaluable tool for re-creating the appropriate sounding part. However, synthesizers have gone well beyond the mere synthesizing of acoustic instruments. And with the vast variety of types of synthesis available today, you can now even create sounds unheard in the natural world.

Developing a solid understanding how synthesis works will help you to fully unlock the true potential of not only Reason's instruments, but also of its effects and utility devices. So let's get started with an overview of sound.

Understanding Sound

Before you can understand the components of a synthesizer, you must first learn the basic elements that compose sound.

Basic Elements of Sound

The basic elements of sound are identified as frequency, timbre, and amplitude.

Frequency

As discussed in the first book, *QuickPro Series: Power in Reason*, sound waves travel in a consecutive series of peaks and troughs. Their frequency is the number of cycles per second measured in units called hertz.

For example, a waveform that has three cycles per second would be translated into written form as 3 hertz or, abbreviated, 3 Hz. A waveform of 1,200 cycles would be written at 1,200 Hz, or 1.2 kilohertz or 1.2 kHz. Human hearing is generally thought to be in the range between 20 Hz and 20 kHz.

Timbre

Most sounds can be broken up to reveal a composite of sine waves at different frequencies. Depending on the frequencies of the waveforms present, the resulting sound can be described as sounding overly bright, buzzlike, clangorous, smooth, round, or any number of similar descriptions. These terms are indicative of the quality of the sound. Often referred to as timbre (pronounced tam-ber), this is also known as the "character" of the sound.

Amplitude

Amplitude is the distance between the high point of a peak and the low point of a trough within the waveform. The unit of measurement used to describe amplitude in the audio realm is called decibels or dB, and is commonly referred to as loudness. Because human hearing is logarithmic, meaning we don't hear all frequencies at the same dB, we are most sensitive to frequencies between the ranges of 250 Hz and 2 kHz. However, note that lower frequencies are required to have higher amplitude, for our ears to perceive them at the same loudness as we do higher frequencies.

The Basic Components of Synthesis

Most synthesizers use the same terminology and design to both create and shape sounds. We'll be focusing on analog subtractive synthesis as the basis for understanding the components and how they reflect the three basic elements of sound. The following circuits are used to create, shape, and even modify sounds. In addition, all the circuits are voltage controlled (CV), which allow for multiple differing circuits to manipulate audio signals.

Don't worry if you find these descriptions even the least bit confusing, as examples of each circuit in the following chapters will provide further amplification.

Voltage-Controlled Oscillator (VCO)

If you were to zoom in on a guitar string after it's been struck or plucked, you'd find the string oscillates, or visibly vibrates. The oscillation of the string forces the air molecules around it to move generating the waves that you perceive aurally as sound. The mass or thickness of the string will determine at what frequency the oscillator vibrates. Thicker strings have a lower frequency of oscillation, whereas thinner strings oscillate at a faster rate.

All synthesizers use an oscillator circuit to generate sound waves. The voltage-control aspect is what determines the frequency or pitch of the oscillator, the higher-voltage settings resulting in higher frequencies. Most synthesizers are capable of generating at least four basic waveforms: sawtooth, square, triangle, and sine waves. Furthermore, some or all of these waveforms are available simultaneously.

Sawtooth Wave

The sawtooth waveform is one that is rich in overtones and harmonics and is generally perceived and described as buzzy and/or bright. It is arguably the most popular of the basic waveforms and is sometimes considered the all-purpose waveform, rendering it most applicable.

Square Wave

The square waveform is often described as having a hollow quality. Like the sawtooth waveform, it contains a lot of harmonic content, yet it sounds quite different in comparison.

Triangle Wave

The triangle waveform has less harmonics and overtones when compared to the sawtooth and square waveforms. It's an ideal waveform for re-creating bass sounds as well as flute tones.

Sine Wave

The sine waveform has no harmonics or overtones and is described as soft in comparison to the others. Sine waves are excellent for sub bass sounds and this is generally how they are applied.

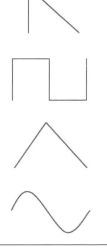

Figure 1.1

Voltage-Controlled Filter (VCF)

The filter circuit of an analog synthesizer is the most important circuit of all, because it differentiates it from any other synthesizer. Filters are used to remove overtones as well as harmonic content.

Types of Filters

There are several filter types, including low-pass, high-pass, band-pass, and notch, all with different slope attributes.

Low-Pass

A low-pass filter (also known as a high-cut filter) removes the higher frequencies and allows the low frequencies to "pass" through.

High-Pass

A high-pass filter (also known as a low-cut filter) removes the low frequencies and allows the higher frequencies to "pass" through.

Band-Pass

A band-pass filter combines both the low- and high-pass filters to allow a central band of frequencies to pass through.

Notch

A notch filter works opposite of a band-pass filter. It instead notches out the central frequencies and leaves both the high and low frequencies to pass through.

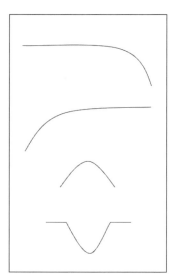

Figure 1.2

Filter Slope

The slope of the filter defines how steep the filter rolls off the frequencies. Slopes are often referred to as poles, each pole representing a 6 dB increment. For instance, the classic Moog filter contains four poles, or a 24 dB increment. The most common filter slopes are two-pole (12 dB) and four-pole (24 dB).

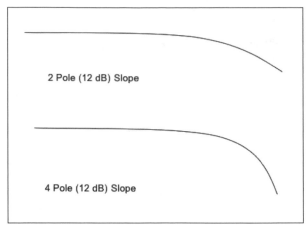

Figure 1.3

Filter Controls

The basic controls of a filter are the Cutoff and Resonance.

Filter Cutoff

The Filter Cutoff control is the point at which the filter starts to remove frequencies. For instance, a low-pass filter with the cutoff set to 450 Hz will start rolling off at frequencies higher than 450 Hz.

Filter Resonance

The Resonance control is essentially a frequency-dependant feedback circuit. When increased, it creates an emphasis at the filter-cutoff frequency. Some filters will launch into self-oscillation when the resonance is increased enough. When using the Filter Cutoff control, this feature becomes tunable feedback. Increasing resonance on a high- or low-pass filter generally results in a thinner sound but creates a sharper, more defined shape. When you are using the notch and band-pass filters, Resonance controls the width of the frequency band so that the higher the setting, the narrower the frequency band will become.

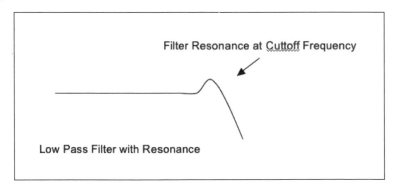

Figure 1.4

Voltage-Controlled Amplifier (VCA)

The voltage-controlled amplifier, in essence, is a preamplifier acting as a volume control. The voltage-control aspect allows for dynamic control over loudness.

Low-Frequency Oscillator (LFO)

The low-frequency oscillator produces various waveforms, like a VCO, but the frequencies are well below human hearing (0.1 Hz to 10 Hz). It is used to create modulation effects as if an invisible hand is physically moving a particular parameter at a given rate and pattern.

LFO Controls

The parameters of an LFO control the rate or frequency, and depth or amplitude.

Rate

The Rate controls the frequency of the LFO so that the higher the rate, the faster the resulting oscillation of the LFO.

Depth

The Depth controls the amplitude of the LFO, which in turn affects how much modulation is sent to the desired circuit. With a lower setting, the resulting modulation is subtle; whereas a higher depth will result in a much more extreme effect.

LFO Effects

Routing the LFO signal to the voltage control of each basic circuit results in three classic effects.

Vibrato
LFO to VCO

Wah-Wah
LFO to VCF

Tremolo
LFO to VCA

Envelope Generator (ADSR)

Using an envelope generator circuit permits the shaping of sound over a period of time. Different stages of the envelope slow or speed up various different signals. Some synthesizers contain a dedicated envelope generator for each circuit, but at the very least there will be one envelope routed to the VCA that controls how a sound is triggered. At its fastest settings, the sound is triggered instantly, whereas slower settings let sounds fade slowly in and out.

The basic stages of an envelope generator are called Attack, Decay, Sustain, and Release. When a particular key is pressed, the level is controlled over time as the sound passes through each stage of the envelope.

Attack

The Attack stage commences when a key is pressed and reflects the time it takes to run upward from 0 to the Decay stage.

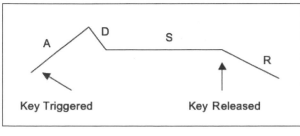

Figure 1.5

Decay

The Decay stage starts at the peak of the Attack stage and continues into the Sustain stage. If the Decay and Sustain are set at the same level, there is no discernable difference between the two.

Sustain

The Sustain stage is the level after the Decay stage and continues until the key being pressed is released.

Release

The Release stage is triggered upon release of the key and is the time taken from the Sustain stage back to 0.

Exploring the Subtractor

Let's now take an in-depth look at the Subtractor synthesizer and examine how all of these circuits work together. We'll cover every aspect of the Subtractor, including most parameters and functions, especially those that are typically found on the majority of the synthesizers found in Reason. This explanation also applies to any hardware or software synth being utilized.

Figure 1.6

Signal Flow

A typical synthesizer's signal flow moves from left to right on the instrument panel, and the Subtractor's signal flow is no exception.

- Once a MIDI note message is received, the upper center section generates sounds via the Oscillator section.
- The audio signal flows from the mix of oscillator into the Filter section.
- Once the signal passes through the Filter section, it continues into the Amp section.
- LFO 1 can be routed to Osc 1 and 2, Osc 2, Freq 1 (of Filter 1), and the mixer.
- LFO 2 can be routed to Osc 1 and 2, Freq 2 (of Filter 2), and the Amp section.
- There are dedicated envelopes for both the Filter 1 and the Amp section.
- The Mod envelope can be routed to Osc 1, Osc 2, mixer, and Freq 2 (of Filter 2).

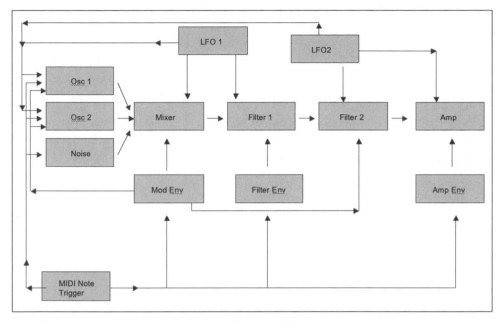

Figure 1.7

Dissecting the Subtractor

Begin by creating a Subtractor, then select Initialize Patch from the Edit menu.

Next, under Filter 1, drag the Freq slider up to 127. This will open up the filter and allow us to hear the oscillators unfiltered.

Subtractor Oscillators 1 and 2

The sounds of the Subtractor begin with the Oscillator section and offer two oscillators as well as a noise source. Press the red button on the upper left corner of Osc 2 and on the noise generator to engage their functions. Both Osc 1 and 2 will exhibit identical functions.

Figure 1.8

Waveforms

By default, the chosen waveform used is the sawtooth. By pressing the upward triangle next to the oscillator waveform, you can scroll through all of the waveforms available for Osc 1.

Following the sawtooth waveform in order are square, triangle, and, lastly, sine wave. First take a listen to the sawtooth and compare it to the square wave, both of which, you will find, sound strong in harmonic content.

Now listen to the triangle and compare it to the sine wave. The triangle waveform contains a lot less harmonic content than do the sawtooth and square waveforms, whereas the sine wave has no harmonics at all.

If you keep pressing the Waveform button, you will notice it starts registering numbers (5–32). Each number represents variations on the waveforms. Some have bell-like qualities, rich in harmonics; others will emulate tones more suitable for brass, strings, mallets, and guitars. For a full description of all the waveforms available, refer to the "Subtractor Oscillator" section of the Reason manual.

Oscillator Tune Controls

Next to the Waveform section, locate the Octave, Semitone, and Cent controls. Each of these is used to change the tuning of the oscillator.

Octave

The Octave section has a range of ten octaves (0–9). Selecting higher settings will cause notes to play at higher pitches, whereas the lower settings will drop the pitch down.

Semitone

Semitones are equivalent to the notes on your MIDI keyboard controller. There are twelve semitones per octave.

Cents

There are one hundred cents per semitone, ranging from –50 to +50. This parameter allows you to fine-tune the pitch, thereby permitting subtle tuning effects as minute as a half-semitone variation up or down.

Kbd Track

When engaged, Keyboard Tracking (Kbd) allows your MIDI keyboard controller to control the pitch; but when disengaged, the oscillator will instead maintain a constant pitch and no control will be possible via the MIDI keyboard controller. This function is particularly useful for creating percussion sounds and special effects.

Phase Control

Creates a second waveform and either multiplies or subtracts it, based on the phase offset.

Phase Knob

Controls the offset of the second waveform.

Mode o

No phase offset.

Mode X

Multiplies the second waveform by the first.

Mode – (Subtract)

This effectively subtracts the second waveform from the first. Setting the Phase knob to 0 while in the Subtract mode causes phase cancellation and no sound will be heard. Moving the Phase knob to any other position will allow the sound to return.

The Phase control may seem a little confusing, but you need not be an expert in the mathematics behind the operation to apply it well. It's quite a valuable tool for creating complex waveforms, as you will learn a little later.

Noise Generator

The noise generator of the Oscillator section creates white noise, which is a useful sound when creating percussion and such sound effects as wind or ocean.

Figure 1.9

Decay

The Decay knob will cause the noise to fade independent of any note or envelope controls.

Color

The Color knob controls the brightness of the noise. Turned to the right, it will create a full blast of white noise; turned to the left, it will cause the sound to become less bright.

Level

The Level knob controls the level of the noise generator.

Oscillator Mix

The Mix knob controls the balance between Osc 1 and 2. Moving the knob fully left will allow only Osc 1 to output, whereas moving it fully to the right allows only Osc 2 to output. When the knob is left in the twelve o'clock position, both Osc 1 and 2 will mix equally. The noise source is routed to the input of Osc 2 on the Mix knob.

FM (Frequency Modulation)

This function is actually a form of synthesis known as FM synthesis or frequency modulation synthesis, which was made popular back in the mid-'80s. Functionally, it allows for Osc 1 to be modulated by Osc 2 or the noise generator, creating unique and sometimes clangorous sounds. You'll explore more about this function in a later section.

Ring Modulator

The ring modulator is another effect that multiplies the sum and difference of both the Osc 1 and 2. The output of this effect can be unpredictable and inharmonic, often resulting in bell-like tones.

Figure 1.10

Subtractor Filters

The Subtractor has two filters, which can be linked to work in tandem or function independently.

Filter 1

Filter 1 is a multimode filter that permits switching between various types of filter.

Figure 1.11

Filter Types

The filter types offered by Subtractor's Filter 1 include Notch, HP 12, BP 12, LP 12, and LP 24.

Notch

The notch filter works as described previously, whereby a frequency band is pulled out according to the Freq slider's position. This is a subtle effect, the sound of which is similar to a phase shift.

HP 12

HP 12 is a 12 dB (two-pole) high-pass filter and will remove low frequencies based on the setting of the Freq slider. With a setting of 0, the filter is open and thereby has no effect on the sound. A setting of 127, however, will remove all the low frequencies from the signal, resulting in a tinny-sounding high-frequency timbre.

BP 12

BP 12 is a 12 dB (two-pole) band-pass filter. Working much like the high- and low-pass filters combined, the result is a narrow band of frequencies. (See Fig. 1.2.) This filter is an excellent choice when layering sounds, as it has proven to be quite versatile with regard to different settings of timbre within the Freq slider.

LP 12

LP 12 is a 12 dB (two-pole) low-pass filter. Setting the Freq slider to 127 will cause the filter to be open and no change in sound will be heard. As the Freq slider is brought down, you will hear the higher frequencies being removed until the 0 point is reached and there's no audible output. The Korg MS20, a popular vintage synthesizer from the 1970s, has a 12 dB filter.

LP 24

LP 24 is a 24 dB (four-pole) low-pass filter. This filter functions just like the LP 12, but has a steeper slope, which removes frequencies at a faster rate. This is a more extreme filter, especially when engaging the Res slider. The Moog Mini-Moog, from the 1970s, has a 24 dB filter and is probably, by far, the most popular synthesizer of all time.

Freq

As stated previously, the Freq slider controls the cutoff frequency of the filter.

Res

Similarly, the Res slider controls the resonance or emphasis of the cutoff frequency. Increasing resonance on a high- or low-pass filter generally results in a thinner sound, but with a sharper, more defined shape. With the notch and band-pass filters, the resonance controls the width of the frequency band. The higher the setting, the narrower the frequency band becomes.

Kbd

This knob controls keyboard tracking, a function that allows the filter to change, depending on which octave of your MIDI keyboard controller you are playing. This function is useful for creating acoustic-sounding instruments, where higher notes are typically brighter. The Kbd knob sets a range of how much the filter opens as you play up the scale of the keyboard.

Filter 2

Filter 2 is identical to Filter 1 set at LP 12. To engage Filter 2, first click the Filter 2 button, which illuminates red when active. The secondary filter has the ability to operate independently. It's arranged in series, which takes its input from the output of Filter 1. When linked, the Freq 1 slider will control Filter 2, but allows for an offset (set by Filter 2's Freq setting). Having two filters permits complex filter effects that would be impossible to achieve with just a single filter.

Level (Amplifier)

The Level slider controls the overall loudness of the instrument and, in essence, is the Amp section. LFO 2 also has an option for modulating the Amp, creating tremolo effects.

Figure 1.12

LFO 1

LFO 1 is a low-frequency oscillator containing various waveforms. With its frequency range well below human hearing, the LFO is never heard, but is used as a modulation source with a variety of destinations.

Waveforms

The Subtractor offers a variety of waveforms, including triangle, upward sawtooth, sawtooth, square, random, and noise.

Figure 1.13

Triangle

The triangle is a smooth-sounding waveform similar to the sine wave.

Upward Sawtooth

The upward sawtooth starts low and rises up to a peak, then repeats the cycle. When set appropriately, it can afford a tape reverse or rewind-like sound.

Sawtooth

The sawtooth starts high and progresses into a falling effect, whereby once the waveform reaches the bottom, it repeats.

Square

The square waveform creates an instantaneous change between up and down. This form is especially useful for creating pseudo-arpeggiator patterns.

Random

The random waveform randomly switches instantaneously between different values and is also known on some analog synthesizers as a sample-and-hold circuit.

Noise

The noise waveform reacts very much like the random, but instead of switching instantaneously between values, it slides smoothly into the next subsequent random value.

LFO 1 Destinations

There are a variety of destinations for LFO 1, including Osc 1 and 2, Osc 2, F. Freq, FM, Phase, and Mix.

Osc 1 and 2

Routing LFO 1 to Osc 1 and 2 creates a vibrato effect by modulating the pitch of both oscillators.

Osc 2

The same as above, but only modulates Osc 2.

F. Freq

This modulates Filter 1's cutoff frequency, thereby creating a wah-wah sound effect.

FM

This modulates the FM (frequency modulation) knob in the Oscillator section. Note, however, both oscillators must be engaged to activate this effect.

Phase

Modulates the phase offset of both oscillators. Either the multiplication or the subtraction must be engaged for this function to work.

Mix

Modulates the Mix control for Osc 1 and 2.

Rate

The Rate knob controls the frequency of the LFO 1. Higher frequencies result in faster modulations.

Sync

The Sync button causes the rate to change from a free-running oscillator (defined by Hz) to synchronize with the tempo of the song. Synchronization is broken into sixteen divisions ranging from 16/4 to 1/32 notes.

Amount

Increasing the Amount knob will increase the amplitude of the LFO. On synths and effects processors, this function is often referred to as Depth. Lower settings are subtler, with higher settings producing more extreme results.

LFO 2

LFO 2 offers a fixed triangle waveform and there's no sync function. It is polyphonic by design, which permits each note to trigger the LFO independently and allows for some interesting rhythmic effects. Most notably is the ability for the LFO's rate to track on the keyboard. Playing higher up the keyboard will result in a faster rate, whereas playing lower notes will generate slower frequencies.

Figure 1.14

LFO 2 Destinations

The destinations for the Subtractor's LFO 2 include Osc 1 and 2, Phase, Filter Freq 2, and Amp.

Osc 1 and 2

Routing LFO 2 to Osc 1 and 2 creates a vibrato effect by modulating the pitch of both oscillators.

Phase

Modulates the phase offset of both oscillators. Note that either the multiplication or subtraction must be engaged for this function to work.

F. Freq 2

Modulates Filter 2's cutoff frequency, creating a wah-wah effect.

Amp
Modulates the Amp section, resulting in a tremolo effect.

Rate
The Rate knob controls the frequency of the LFO 2. Higher frequencies result in faster modulations.

Amount
Increasing the Amount knob will increase the amplitude of the LFO. On synths and effects processors, this function is often referred to as Depth. The lower settings produce more subtle results, whereas while the higher settings will produce more extreme results.

Delay
LFO 2 Delay generates a delay between the time a note is played and the modulation of the desired parameter. This is useful when playing keyboard parts because the modulation will only occur on sustained notes.

Kbd
LFO 2 Keyboard Tracking (Kbd) allows the LFO to follow the keyboard, with higher notes resulting in faster rates, whereas lower notes generate slower frequencies.

Envelope Generators
As discussed previously, envelopes allow the control of parameters over time, with Attack, Decay, Sustain, and Release (ADSR) being the parameters that shape the sound. The Subtractor features two dedicated envelopes for the Amp and Filter 1 circuits. An additional envelope, Modulation (Mod env), has a number of different destinations that can result in some pretty spectacular effects.

Amp Env
The Amplifier envelope allows for the dynamic control over loudness. With longer attacks and releases, you can create slowly evolving sounds that will fade in and out. Decay adds an addition dynamic portion to the cycle, and Sustain holds its value indefinitely until the key is released.

Figure 1.15

Filter Env
The Filter envelope allows for the dynamic control over the cutoff frequency of Filter 1 over time. Additional parameters include Invert and Envelope Amount.

Amount
The Envelope Amount control makes it possible to dial in just how much the envelope will affect Filter 1's frequency cutoff. Having a lower setting on the Filter 1 while increasing the amount using the knob will result in Filter 1's frequency to increase dynamically over time.

Figure 1.16

Invert
The Invert button flips the envelope; instead of increasing Filter 1's frequency over time, the envelope will lessen, thereby causing the filter to close.

Mod Env
The Modulation envelope allows you to control multiple destinations or parameters over time.

Figure 1.17

Osc 1

Routing the Mod envelope to Osc 1 will increase the pitch dynamically over time. Engage the Invert button to have the pitch drop over time. This effect is made popular in DrumNbass, which has huge bass tones that slowly drop in pitch.

Osc 2

Functions the same as Osc 1.

FM

This is used to dynamically change the FM (frequency modulation) parameter in the Osc section. Note that both oscillators must be active for this effect to be heard.

Phase

Use this to dynamically change the phase offset of the Osc 1 and 2 over time.

Freq 2

The Filter envelope allows for the dynamic control over the cutoff frequency of Filter 2 over time.

Amount

Amount allows you to dial in how much the envelope will affect the selected parameters. Lower settings will be subtler, whereas higher settings will result in a more extreme effect.

Invert

The Invert button flips the envelope; instead of increasing a selected parameter over time, it decreases.

Velocity

Velocity by definition is the speed at something moves, happens, or is done. We often equate this speed with the strength of which we play a note on our MIDI keyboard controller.

Figure 1.18

The Subtractor features comprehensive control over parameters with velocity. A typical control of velocity is the control of level or volume: the harder a key is struck; the louder the sound will be generated. With the dials set at twelve o'clock, the function is bypassed. Moving a parameter to the right causes a positive function, whereas moving it to the left produces a negative effect.

Amp

Velocity control of the amp circuit results in dynamic control of volume. A positive setting produces the typical result in which, the harder a key is played, the louder the sound output. Negative values result in the opposite of this function, whereby the harder pressed keys are softer in volume and softer hit keys are played louder.

FM

Velocity control over the FM (frequency modulation) parameter of the Oscillator section results in an increase of the FM setting at a positive value. A negative value results in the opposite reaction. Note that both Osc 1 and 2 must be active, to use this function.

M. Env

Velocity control over the Mod Env results in an increase over the Mod Env amount at a positive value. A negative value results in the opposite reaction.

Phase

Velocity control over the phase parameter of the Oscillator section results in an increase over the phase offset at a positive value. A negative value results in the opposite reaction.

Freq 2

Velocity control over the Freq 2 results in an increase over Filter 2's filter cutoff frequency at a positive value. A negative value results in the opposite reaction.

F. Env

Velocity control over the Filter Env results in an increase over Filter 1's envelope amount at a positive value. A negative value results in the opposite reaction.

F. Dec

Velocity control over the Filter Env Decay results in an increase over Decay portion of the Filter 1's decay time of the envelope at a positive value. A negative value results in the opposite reaction.

Mix

Velocity control over the Oscillator Mix parameter results in an increase over the Osc 2's mix amount at a positive value. A negative value results in an increase over the Osc 1's mix amount.

A. Atk

Velocity control over the Amp envelope Attack (A. Atk) results in an increase over the attack portion of the amp's Attack time of the envelope at a positive value. A negative value results in the opposite reaction.

Pitch Bend and Modulation Wheel

Most MIDI keyboard controllers offer real-time control over pitch bend and modulation via dedicated wheels. These parameters are routed to the onscreen Pitch Bend and Modulation wheels.

Bend

The Pitch Bend wheel permits bending notes by set intervals.

Figure 1.19

Range

Pitch Bend Range sets the range of the Pitch Bend wheel. The maximum setting range is twenty-four semitones, or two octaves.

Mod

The Modulation wheel is assignable to a number of parameters. Setting the knob at twelve o'clock has no effect and causes it, in essence, to be bypassed. Moving the knob to the right will cause the function to work in a positive manner, whereas moving the knob to the left will cause a negative or inverted reaction. All functions can be assigned simultaneously, which affords very complex sound manipulation with a simple movement of the wheel.

F. Freq

Assigns the Mod wheel to Filter 1's frequency cutoff. A positive setting causes the filter to open up, whereas a negative setting will cause the filter to close.

F. Res

Assigns the Mod wheel to Filter 1's Resonance control. A positive setting increases resonance, whereas a negative setting will decrease it.

LFO 1

Assigns the Mod wheel to LFO 1's Amount knob. A positive setting increases the amount, whereas a negative setting decreases it.

Phase

Assigns the Mod wheel to the Phase Offset parameter of both Osc 1 and 2. A multiplication or subtraction setting must be activated for the parameter to work.

FM

Assigns the Mod wheel to the FM (frequency modulation) of the Oscillator section. A positive setting will increase the FM amount, whereas a negative setting will decrease it. Note that both oscillators must be activated for the parameter to work.

Ext. Mod

The External Modulation section allows you to control certain parameters with the use of common MIDI messages. To use this function, first select the type of incoming message the Subtractor should respond to, then set the range of parameters from the following options.

Common MIDI Messages

Figure 1.20

There are three common MIDI messages: Aftertouch, Expression, and Breath. Once selected, these messages are routed to various destinations.

A. Touch

A MIDI keyboard controller typically transmits Aftertouch. Most keyboards employ monophonic Aftertouch, whereby a single sensor runs the span of the keyboard. When a key is pressed with continuous pressure, a controller message is generated. The harder the key is pressed, the greater the value generated. Values range from 0 to 127.

Expr.

Expression control (Expr.) is often employed by the use of an Expression pedal. These types of pedals are found in most music retailers and generate a range from 0 to 127.

Breath

A Breath controller is usually employed by use of a MIDI Wind controller with a pressure sensor. Blowing into the unit will generate a range from 0 to 127.

External Modulation Destinations

The external modulation destinations include Filter Frequency Cutoff (F. Freq), LFO 1, Amp, and FM.

F. Freq

Positive values will increase Filter 1's frequency cutoff, whereas a negative will invert the signal, causing the cutoff to decrease.

LFO 1

Positive values will increase LFO 1's amount parameter, whereas a negative will invert the signal causing the cutoff to decrease.

Amp

Positive values will increase the volume of the instrument, whereas a negative will invert the signal causing the volume to decrease.

FM

Positive values will increase the FM (frequency modulation) amount of the Oscillator section, whereas a negative will invert the signal, causing the FM amount to decrease.

Play Parameters

Play parameters allow the user to define how the Subtractor will react to incoming MIDI messages.

Note On

The purpose of this LED is to let you know that the instrument is receiving MIDI messages.

Legato

Legato is a mode typical to analog synthesizers, especially monophonic synths. This mode prevents an envelope from retriggering unless the key is released. When using with more than one voice, it won't activate until all the allocated voices have been used.

Retrig

Retrigger has two functions, the first of which is used when playing polyphonic patches. In this situation, it retriggers the envelopes regardless of the number of keys held or voices allocated. The retrigger's second function is designed to work like most monophonic synthesizers. If one note is pressed followed simultaneously by a second, the envelope is retriggered. If the second note is release, the first held note is retriggered.

Portamento

Portamento is a glide between notes, instead of jumping instantaneously to the next pitch. The Portamento knob is used to control how long the glide will take for it to reach the new pitch. A setting of 0 results in no portamento effect.

Polyphony

Polyphony is defined as the number of voices (or keys) that can be played simultaneously. A setting of 1 defines the synth as monophonic, or one note at a time. Settings from 2 to 99 will allow up the designated number of voices to play. Note that if Polyphony is set to 5 and then six notes are played, the first note played will be stolen, or removed, to play the sixth.

Low BW

The Low Bandwidth button is designed to conserve the CPU. When activated, the high frequency of a sound is removed.

Programming Custom Patches with the Subtractor

Now let's take a closer look at some basic programming of synth patches, using the Subtractor.

If you haven't done so already, first create a Subtractor.

Next, initialize the patch by selecting Initialize from the Edit menu and bring Filter 1's Freq slider up to 127.

Standard Effects

Standard effects found on basic effects processors are vibrato, wah-wah, and tremolo.

Vibrato

To create a vibrato effect, route LFO 1 to Osc 1 and 2 (set by default) and increase the amount to 50. Try different waveforms on LFO 1 to hear how they affect the modulation.

Wah-Wah

To create a wah-wah effect, route LFO 1 to F. Freq. Lower Filter 1's Freq slider to 80. Try raising the Res slider to 70 and try out the different types of filters.

Tremolo

To create a tremolo, initialize the patch and bring Filter 1's Freq slider to 127.

Set LFO 2's destination to Amp and increase the amount to 127.

PWM

Pulse width modulation (PWM) is a fantastic way to introduce motion into a static oscillator's waveform.

A standard square wave has a fifty-fifty relationship between the up and down portions of the waveform. A pulse wave is like a square wave, but the up and down portions' relationship is something other than fifty-fifty. By modulating the phase offset of a square wave, you can create pulse width modulation (PWM), which will create harmonic motion by modulating the pulse of the square wave.

- Initialize the patch and bring Filter 1's Freq slider to 127.
- Begin by changing Osc 1 to a square wave and set the phase to subtraction.
- Next, set LFO 1's destination to phase and increase Amount to 87 and Rate to 52.

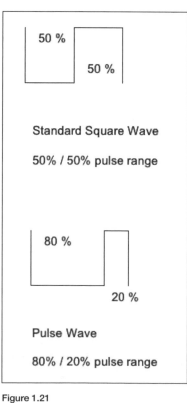

Figure 1.21

Lead

With the PWM you've just created, let's create a lead sound.

- Turn on Osc 2 and increase the semitone to 5.
- Turn the FM knob to 24.
- Bring the Decay and Sustain sliders of the Amp envelope to 127.

Bass Drop

Initialize the patch and bring Filter 1's Freq slider to 127.

- Set Osc 1's waveform to a sine wave and lower the octave to 3.
- Set the Decay and Sustain sliders of the Amp envelope to 127.
- Lower Polyphony to 1.
- On the Mod envelope, make sure that Osc 1 is selected.
- Set Attack to 110 and lower Decay to 0.
- Select the Invert button and increase the amount to 127.

Final Thoughts

It is my belief that much of sound design is effectively and, often simply, done through careful and repeated experimentation. Once you fully understand the basics of synthesis and grasp its function, it won't be long before you'll be able to hear a sound in your head and replicate it by using the synthesizer. Another great method of learning synth programming is to study other presets and apply similar programming to your own custom patches.

In the next chapter, you will explore the Thor Polysonic Synthesizer and the Malstrom Graintable Synthesizer.

Chapter 2
REASON INSTRUMENTS

Thor Polysonic Synthesizer

Synthesizers, or synths, from their earliest commercial production, were produced in modular form. Moog and Buchla were among the first manufacturers to release synthesizers of this format. A modular synthesizer consists of a number of modules with each containing a circuit used to provide a specific function. Patch cables are used to route the audio and control voltage signals between the different modules. This modular approach allowed for the ultimate in expression and flexibility, enabling musicians to create and process audio in a near-infinite number of ways. However, most modular synths of this time were quite large, very expensive, and not easily transported.

In 1970, Moog developed the MiniMoog synthesizer, a much more compact unit designed to target the performing musician. This synthesizer was sold preconfigured and prewired, thereby eliminating the need for patch cabling.

Another manufacturer, Alan R. Pearlman, created the Arp 2600 in the mid- to late '70s, introducing a unique semimodular design. This synth came preconfigured and prewired, but also offered patch points with which to reroute the prewired signals, thus providing the superior flexibility of the early modular synthesizers.

The Thor Polysonic synthesizer was designed as a semimodular synthesizer. It features the additional ability to swap out different modules, each containing a different and unique character. The result is a synthesizer design that is both complex and yet extremely simple to use.

The Thor is broken up into four sections: the Controller panel, the Programmer, the Modulation Routing section, and the Step Sequencer.

Figure 2.1

The Controller Panel

The Controller panel contains the familiar Pitch Bend and Mod wheel controls as well as Patch selection and Master Volume control. In addition, it offers three control sections: Keyboard Modes, Trigger, and assignable controls.

Figure 2.2

Keyboard Modes

The Keyboard Modes section controls how Thor responds to incoming MIDI messages.

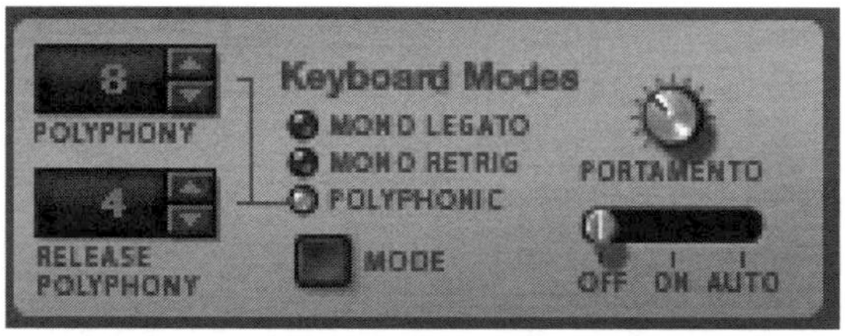

Figure 2.3

Polyphony

Sets the number of voices (up to thirty-two) that can be played simultaneously.

Polyphony Release

Sets the number of voices that will decay following the release section of the envelopes. As new notes are played, the previously played notes will continue to play out. If 0 is selected, the release is cut off when a new note is played.

Mono Legato

Prevents the envelope from retriggering when new notes are played. When selected, this function works regardless of the settings selected in the Polyphony setting.

Mono Retrigger

Causes notes to retrigger when new notes are played.

Portamento

Causes notes to slide into the next pitch value instead of playing the new pitch instantaneously.

On/Off/Auto

Sets the Portamento mode to either On, Off, or Auto. The Auto setting will only activate portamento when more than one note is held.

Figure 2.4

Trigger Section

Allows for sounds to be triggered by both notes and the sequencer. Both can be activated simultaneously.

Assignable Controls

These two knobs and two buttons are assignable to any parameter via the Modulation Routing section. Multiple parameters can be assigned simultaneously. The buttons offer note assignments and will act as momentary switches when notes are triggered via the MIDI controller keyboard.

Figure 2.5

The Programmer

The programmer serves as the heart of the instrument and features both sound creation and manipulation functionality. It contains two sections, Voice and Global.

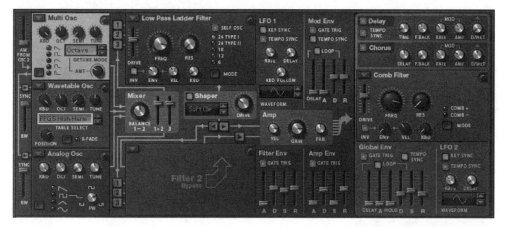

Figure 2.6

Voice Section

The Voice section generates waveforms via three oscillators.

Oscillators 1, 2, and 3

The Thor offers six types of oscillators that are selectable from the downward triangle in the upper left corner of each oscillator. Each oscillator offers the same familiar controls as you're accustomed to from the Subtractor and includes Keyboard Tracking, Octave, Semitone, and Tune (Cents). Beyond that, each oscillator features the ability to vary drastically, thereby affording a broad tonal pallet. Oscillators 2 and 3 offer oscillator sync to Oscillator 1.

Analog

This oscillator offers the same basic waveforms as found in the Subtractor. These waveforms include sawtooth, square (with PWM), triangle, and sine.

Figure 2.7

Wavetable

Wavetable synthesis was the precursor to the advent of the sampler and was made popular by the Korg Wavestation, PPG Wave, and Waldorf Wave. A wavetable is a digital oscillator consisting of thirty-two wavetables, each with sixty-four waves, each wavetable offering a unique tonal palette.

Figure 2.8

Position Knob

The Position knob allows you to dial in a specific waveform pattern within the waveform itself. You can also modulate the Position knob from the Modulation Control section, which causes the sound to sweep through the wavetable.

X-Fade

When engaged, an X-Fade (cross-fade) is placed between each wave in the wavetable, causing the sweep to become smooth. With the X-Fade off, the sweep will instead jump to the next wave with an audible effect.

Phase Modulation

Phase modulation is also known as phase distortion synthesis. The Phase Modulation oscillator causes two waveforms to play in series, so the phase interplays between the two, creating the effect of filter manipulation. When two waveforms are active, the second waveform generated is positioned one octave below the fundamental of the first. This technology was first pioneered by Korg, but made famous by the Casio CZ series synthesizers.

Figure 2.9

PD Knob

Changes the shape of the waveform.

FM Pair

Frequency modulation (FM) synthesis uses slightly different terminology but is conceptually the same as analog synthesis, in which one oscillator modulates another oscillator. In FM, the modulating oscillators are referred to as operators.

The FM pair is a scaled-down and simplified version of its larger, more complex brethren usually found on hardware/software synthesizers, such as the Yamaha DX7 and Native Instruments FM7.

In Reason, the two are referred to as oscillators, not operators.

Figure 2.10

Carrier

This is the first oscillator and is modulated by the modulator oscillator.

Modulator

This is the second oscillator and modulates the carrier oscillator.

FM Knob

Controls the amount of frequency modulation.

Multi Oscillator

The multi oscillator has the ability to generate multiple detuned waves.

By your selecting a basic waveform and the mode of detuning, the oscillator will generate a copy and detune it in various ways. The Amount knob controls how much detuning occurs. This particular oscillator is ideal for creating bell-like tones and cymbal sounds. Check the patch library under Percussion > Cymbals for examples.

Figure 2.11

Noise

The Noise oscillator offers multiple types of noise and has dedicated controls, each having a different effect on the chosen noise selection. It can generate pure white noise or various styles of colored noise, each possessing a unique characteristic. This unit may be used as a pitch oscillator or a modulation source.

Figure 2.12

Band

Band noise, with BW control, allows for the fine-tuning of the bandwidth. Positioning the knob fully clockwise allows for a wide band of noise, whereas moving the knob counterclockwise narrows the band.

S/H

Sample and Hold are found on many vintage synths and produce a type of randomization. The Rate control, when positioned fully clockwise, offers a wide spectrum of noise akin to white noise. As the knob is moved counterclockwise, you start to hear the random pulses generated from the noise. This can be used to great effect at lower rates as a modulation source for other oscillators.

Static

Static is exactly as it sounds. The Density knob, when positioned fully clockwise, offers a wide-range noise. As the knob is moved counterclockwise, you begin to hear the static noise breaking up. At lower settings it sounds much like a dirty stylus cracking and popping on a turntable.

Color

Colored noise offers a wide range of noise tones to use. The Color knob, when positioned fully clockwise, affords an emphasis on high-frequency noise, whereas moving the knob counterclockwise increasingly emphasizes the low-frequency noise.

White

White noise is offered where all frequencies are positioned at the same amplitude. There is no knob for this as all frequencies are equal.

Filters 1 and 2

There are two identical, dedicated filter slots in the Voice section, offering a total of four filter types each. The filters may be run in series or parallel. All the filters have the familiar common parameters found on most synthesizers, which include Filter Cutoff, Filter Resonance, Kbd for filter tracking, Velocity, Invert, and a Drive function that allows for the overdriving of the filter's input, which brings out more character in the filter.

It must be noted that the filter section of any synthesizer is the most important factor to consider in determining the character of a particular synthesizer. For example, this is what makes a Moog sound like a Moog. In fact, this element is so crucial there was a time where many manufacturers were suing one another over "stolen" filter designs.

Low-Pass Ladder Filter

This filter design was faithfully modeled after a Moog Ladder Filter, which refers to the circuit design that visually resembles a ladder. It provides a warm, musical sound and is probably the most popular filter design today. It is capable of self-oscillation via a dedicated button, which allows for the filter to act as tuned feedback. The filter also offers four different slopes or poles: 6 dB, 12 dB, 18 dB, and two variations on 24 dB.

Figure 2.13

24 dB Type I
Sets the drive function at the filter output before the feedback loop input.

24 dB Type II
Sets the drive function at the filter input after the feedback loop.

Both types also offer unique sounds when the Self-oscillation button is engaged. The resonance and feedback, however, are more pronounced with Type I.

State Variable Filter

The state variable filter is modeled after the Oberheim SEM synthesizer and offers a warm, creamy sound.

Figure 2.14

This multimode filter, which will self-oscillate via the dedicated button, has LP, BP, HP, Notch, and Peak settings. Both the Notch and Peak settings have a dedicated knob for toggling between the High-Pass and Low-Pass settings. When the knob is set at 12 o'clock, the filter functions as either Notch or Peak. This allows for smooth transitions to different filter types and can be used as a modulation source.

Comb Filter

This unique filter adds a series of short delays to the original signal. Each delay is a narrow band that visually resembles the teeth of a comb when viewed on an oscilloscope.

Figure 2.15

The comb filter offers unique phasing sounds with subtle pitch variations. The filter will generate tunable feedback with high-resonance settings coupled with low-frequency cutoff.

The Comb's – (minus) setting will cut or remove low frequencies from the signal.

Formant Filter

The formant filter has the ability to generate vowel sounds, thus enabling the creation of talking synth patches.

Figure 2.16

There is no filter cutoff or resonance. Instead, this filter uses a control pad with X and Y axes to control parameters. It has a frequency shift labeled Gender, which can add female or male characteristics to the voicelike sounds it generates.

Shaper

The shaper circuit takes input from Filter 1's output and is designed to enable reshaping of the incoming signal.

Figure 2.17

Subtle amounts of shaping will add warmth, whereas the extreme settings will generate heavily distorted sounds.

Following the signal flow, the shaper can be routed to either Filter 2, which allows for the filters to be run in series, or to the Amp section.

Amp

The Amp, or amplifier, section receives sounds exiting the Filter section before the signal enters the Global section.

Figure 2.18

It has a dedicated Gain knob and a knob for controlling how the amplifier responds to incoming velocity information. The Amp section also has a dedicated Pan knob that moves the sound to different points in the stereo field. It is possible to modulate this parameter to cause different voices to sound as if they are moving about dynamically within the stereo field.

LFO 1

LFO 1 functions just like the LFO on the Subtractor, with additional waveforms.

However, this LFO is polyphonic, which means it will generate a new cycle with each voice triggered (up to the maximum number afforded by the polyphony setting). It has the same basic controls, such as Waveform selection, Rate, and Tempo sync; in addition, it also offers Keysync, Kbd Follow, and Delay controls.

Keysync

Forces any new cycle of the LFO to begin at the start of the waveform. When disengaged, the LFO is free running and might initiate anywhere within the cycle of the waveform.

Figure 2.19

KBD Follow

This function allows the LFO to track the keyboard. The higher the notes are played on the MIDI controller keyboard, the faster the rate will become.

Delay

Adds a delayed response from the triggered voice and when the LFO begins modulating. This is great for adding motion effects on sustained notes, whereas shorter notes are left unaffected.

Envelopes

There are three envelopes in the Voice section of the Thor programmer. Its dedicated Filter envelope and Amplifier envelope function just as do the ADSR parameters in the Subtractor. By default, these envelopes are triggered by note on messages. But they can also be triggered by any other parameter by disengaging the Gate Trigger button and assigning the envelope trigger to another source via the Modulation Routing section.

The third envelope, called the Mod Env, is only assigned from the Modulation Routing section and can be set to control any assignable parameter. It includes the standard ADSR controls, but also has some additional parameters, such as Delay, Loop, and Tempo Sync.

Delay

Controls the time before the envelope will effect the desired parameter.

Figure 2.20

Loop

This causes the Delay to the Decay to loop, or repeat, indefinitely.

Tempo Sync

When activated, this setting allows for each stage of the envelope to lock to the global tempo of the song. The Sync setting ranges from 1/32 to 4/1.

Global Section

The Global section of the Thor synthesizer adds a third filter, a second LFO, an expanded envelope, and two effects processors.

The Filter and LFO have the same functionality as the other filters and LFOs as discussed previously in this chapter.

Figure 2.21

The Effects section offers a dedicated Delay function with tempo sync, modulation, and rate controls, as well as a dedicated Chorus effect.

The Global envelope offers some additional controls beyond the standard ADSR. Just like the Mod Env, the Global Env offers Delay, Loop, Tempo Sync, and Gate Trigger, with an additional Hold stage within the envelope, which "holds" for a predetermined amount of time before continuing on to the Decay stage of the envelope.

The Modulation Routing Section

This section serves as the nerve center of the instruments, which allows you to route audio and CV signals to various destinations. It's broken up into three subsections.

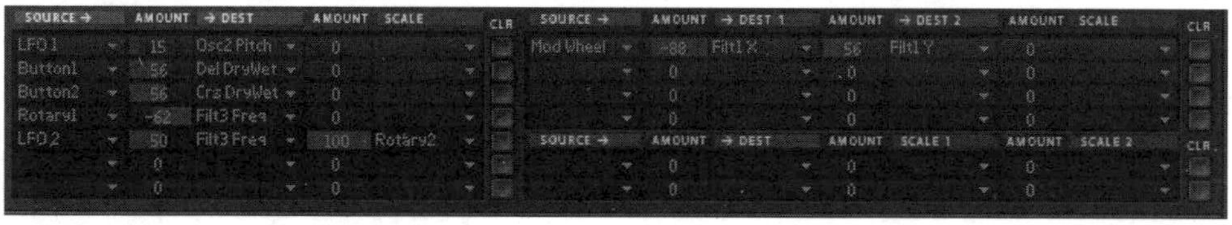

Figure 2.22

On the left side, you'll see seven rows of five columns. The title of each column is written across the top: Source > Amount > Destination > Amount > Scale.

Let's look at a simple example.

Start by creating a Thor Synthesizer. Initialize the patch by selecting Initialize from the Edit menu.

Next, in the Modulation Routing section, select LFO 1 under the Source column. Then, under the Destination column, select Filter Frequency.

Finally, after setting the amount to 100, play a note on your MIDI controller keyboard. You will hear the filter being modulated by LFO 1.

Now, under the Scale column, select Performance > Mod Wheel and increase the amount displayed to 100. The Scale function allows you to control the depth, or amount of the LFO, using the Mod wheel. Play a note and raise the setting of the Mod wheel to hear the modulation increase as the Mod wheel is moved. Next drag the setting of the Mod wheel down to −100. As this number decreases, less LFO 1 is sent to the filter.

Let's now take a look at the two other modulation sections. These work the same as the previous modulation section, with the notable exception of additional columns.

The section on the upper right offers four rows of seven columns: Source > Amount > Dest 1 > Amount > Dest 2 > Amount > Scale.

This section allows you to modulate two destinations from a single source. The Scale function affects both destinations simultaneously.

The section on the lower right offers two rows of seven columns: Source > Amount > Dest > Amount > Scale 1 > Amount > Scale 2.

This section allows for two scale functions to control the amount of the source being routed to the destination simultaneously.

The Step Sequencer

Thor's Step Sequencer design harks back to the days of the analog sequencers. It features sixteen steps with a variety of output data that can be generated simultaneously. When combined with the Modulation Routing section, it becomes a veritable powerhouse of creativity.

Figure 2.23

Let's proceed with a quick tutorial to get things running. This will be followed by a deeper explanation of all the individual controls.

- To activate the sequencer, make sure to have the Step Seq button activated in the Trigger section of the Controller panel.
- Next, select Repeat from the Run Mode options on the left side of the interface and click the Run button.
- The sequencer will start running and you should hear a constant sixteenth-note pattern.
- The right side of the sequencer is the Step Edit section, which contains sixteen knobs and buttons. The knobs allow you to dial in specific note values, whereas the buttons, when deactivated, create rests.
- Create rests at Steps 4, 8, and 12.
- Set knobs 2, 6, 10, and 14 to G2. Set knob 16 to C#3.
- You should now have a sequence that looks like this:

Figure 2.24

Now that you have a basic sequence running, let's examine some of the other options available on the Step Sequencer.

Run Mode

Run Mode controls how the sequencer operates. Options include Repeat, 1-Shot, and Step.

Repeat

Selecting this option causes the sequencer to play indefinitely.

1 Shot

Selecting this option will cause the sequencer to play through once and stop.

Step

Selecting this will cause the sequencer to play each step with a corresponding incoming note message.

Direction

The Direction function controls whether the sequencer runs forward, backward, randomly, or in a pendulum.

Forward

The sequence will run from left to right.

Reverse

The sequence will run from right to left.

Pendulum 1

This helps keep the sequence locked into its intended grid value. The sequence will run from left to right and right to left. The first and last steps will play twice.

Pendulum 2

This is almost the same setting as Pendulum 1, except that the first and last steps are not repeated.

Random

Randomly jumps around throughout the sequence.

Rate

The Rate section can be set to run freely or lock to note values ranging from 1/64 to 16/4.

Edit

The Edit section allows for the sequencing of multiple types of data. Editing is directly related to the sixteen knobs in the Step Edit section. The types of data sequencing include Note, Velocity, Gate Length, Step Duration, Curve 1, and Curve 2.

Note sequencing contains an Octave switch for scaling knob values to two octaves, four octaves, and full range.

Curves 1 and 2 offer similar controls to those found in the Matrix pattern sequencer curve controls.

Edit selections are available from within the Modulation Routing section of the Thor sequencer.

Steps

The Thor sequencer offers up to sixteen steps per sequence, but that number may be further decreased to create shorter sequences. This is achieved by clicking on the LEDs above the knob in the Step Edit section.

Note Transposing Sequence

One of my favorite uses for the Step Sequencer is to control the transposition via incoming MIDI notes. Use the following steps to try this out.

- First, lower the Polyphony setting to one voice.
- In the left section of the Modulation Routing section, select MIDI Key > Gate from the first row of the Source column. Increase the amount to 100.
- In the destination column, select Step Sequencer > Trigger.
- In the second row, select MIDI Key > Note from the Source column. Increase the amount to 100.
- In the destination column, select Step Sequencer > Transpose.
- Now, the sequencer is triggered and transposed by any note selected on the MIDI keyboard controller.

Malstrom Graintable Synthesizer

The Malstrom synthesizer is wholly unique due to its implementation of a new type of synthesis called Graintable. This effectively combines both granular and wavetable synthesis to create a sound that is more than the sum of its parts.

Granular synthesis is incredibly complex and involves the generation of grains of sound by either mathematical formula or sampled waveforms. The individual grains are manipulated by changing the pitch, order, speed, and format of each grain.

Wavetable synthesis, as discussed in the Thor Oscillator section, consists of banks of short sampled waveforms that contain various types of harmonically rich tones, which are all sweepable by means of various modulation sources.

By combining the simplicity of wavetable selection and the complexity of sound manipulation from Graintable, you are able to create sounds unique that cannot be produced by any other type of synthesis.

By now, you should have a good understanding of synthesis and how all the circuits and parameters interact with each other. Therefore, instead of rehashing a description of each individual component of the instrument interface, let's instead explore the unique aspects of the synthesizer.

Osc A and B

The heart and soul of the Malstrom is the Oscillator section. Each of the two oscillators contains the already familiar pitch adjustment parameters, including Octave, Semitone, and Cent, as well as dedicated amplifier envelopes.

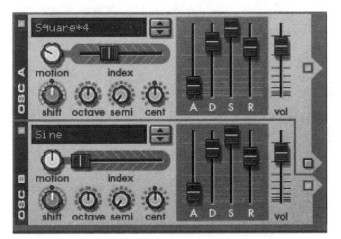

Figure 2.25

Each oscillator may be switched on or off by simply selecting the square in the upper left corner. Select a wavetable by either clicking on the name of the waveform in the drop-down box, or by using the up/down arrows to select the desired waveform. The variety of available waveforms is quite extensive and ranges from Bass, FX, Guitars, and Percussion to Synths, Voice, Waves, and Wind.

Once a desired waveform is selected, there are three granular controls—Index, Motion, and Shift—to further manipulate the sound.

Index

The Index control allows you to select a specific point within the graintable to initiate the sound. At the left side of the slider, the sound begins with the first grain and moves to the right. Simply adjust the index slider to select a different starting point. This really comes into play when utilizing complex waveforms that can drastically change the mood and feeling of your patch.

Motion

Each graintable has a preprogrammed motion pattern, that moves either forward or forward and backward. The patterns are predetermined for each graintable and are not able to be edited. However, the Motion knob can be used to control how quickly the sound cycles through the index. At the 12 o'clock position, it runs at its normal rate, whereas moving the knob to the right increases the speed, and moving it to the left decreases the speed. If the knob is rotated all the way to the left, the waveform becomes static. You'll also notice that the speed of motion will track across the keyboard so that higher notes will have faster speeds.

Shift

The Shift knob, much like the Formant Filter of the Thor, controls the formant of the sound and can dramatically alter its harmonic content. It essentially adjusts the pitch of each individual grain, not the pitch of the overall graintable.

Routing Oscillators

There are triangular points that indicate routing on the Malstrom. These, coupled with the ability to bypass any circuit, allows for easy-to-follow, very flexible routing capabilities.

Osc A is routed through the Wave Shaper circuit and then onto Filter A. Osc A can also be routed through Filter B, a final destination, or through the Wave Shaper and Filter A.

Osc B is routed through Filter B, but can be routed through the Wave Shaper and Filter A as well.

By not engaging the routing buttons, it is possible to route the sound directly to the output, bypassing all available circuits.

Filters A and B

Both Malstrom filters are multimode and contain LP 12, BP 12, Comb +, Comb –, and AM, all of which were explained in the Thor section.

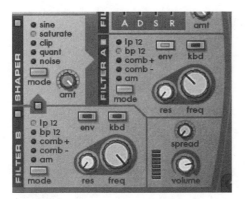

Figure 2.26

There are the usual Freq Cutoff and Resonance controls, as well as dedicated buttons for keyboard tracking and for engaging the dedicated Filter envelope.

Modulation (Mod A and B)

The Mod A and B section, which is essentially the LFO section, is used to create modulation effects.

Figure 2.27

Both sections contain a vast array of waveforms, well beyond the standard sawtooth, square, triangle, and sine. Both sections also have the ability to synchronize to the tempo of a song. The 1-Shot button allows the Mods to cycle through the given waveform once, effectively engaging them for use as pseudo-envelopes. Mod A or B can modulate the oscillator and filter A and B either together or separately by setting the A/B selector switch.

Mod A

Mod A contains destinations to Pitch, Index, and Shift.

Mod B

Mod B contains destinations for Motion, Volume, Filter, and Mod A.

Performance Control

This is the already familiar type of interface that you've seen on both the Subtractor and Thor synthesizers. It contains the usual assortment of controls with additional dedicated options for Polyphony and Portamento.

Velocity

The Velocity section offers control over the levels of both the A and B sections, as well as the Filter envelope. In addition, there is independent control over the A and B sections for the Attack (Amp envelope), Shift, and Modulation settings.

Pitch Bend and Mod Wheel

The Pitch Bend range can be set up to twenty-four semitones, spanning a total of four octaves.

The Mod wheel maintains independent control over the A and B sections for Index, Shift, Filter, and Modulation.

Wobble Bass Patch

Let's look at how to program a wobble bass; often used in Dubstep, Crunk, DrumNbass, and other forms of Bass Culture electronic dance music.

Make sure you have a mixer already set up, as you will be utilizing two separate outputs for this patch.

Start by creating a Malstrom and select initialize from the Edit menu.

Next, turn on Osc B.

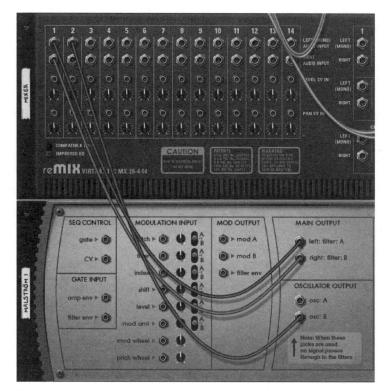

Figure 2.28

- Tab to the back of the interface and cable Osc B from the Oscillator Output section to Channel 2 on the mixer.
- Next, from the Osc A graintable section, select SweepingSquare from the list of available waveforms.
- Set the Index of Osc A to 38.
- Set Osc A Shift to –4.
- Set the Release of both Osc A and Osc B to 83.
- Set Osc B Octave to 3.
- Engage the Shaper circuit. Select Saturate and increase the amount to 127.
- Set the Freq knob to 46 on Filter A. Select BP12.
- Set the waveform in Mod B to a triangle and increase the Filter knob setting to 47.

Figure 2.29

The Wobble Bass patch created should look like the image shown. Save this patch for now so it can be utilized later during in the advanced sequencing chapter.

Chapter 3
SAMPLING

What Is a Sampler?

A sampler is, in essence, a synthesizer that utilizes recorded samples of audio instead of using oscillators. The sampler, as a production tool, affords an unprecedented amount of creative freedom. With it, you can record, process, and play any sound within the confines of an instrument, thereby offering unlimited sonic possibilities.

Samplers and sample playback devices add a new level of realism to music production. Instead of using a synthesizer to approximate the sounds of strings, brass, pianos, bass, or any other acoustic instrument, you instead use recorded waveforms of those actual instruments.

A Brief History of the Sampler

The earliest samplers were keyboard-driven tape instruments. The most popular of these was the Mellotron, which gained notoriety in the late '60s. This sampler used prerecorded material recorded onto magnetic tape. These units were fairly expensive and fragile, and required a lot of maintenance due to the eventual and ever-constant need to replace the recorded tape.

The mid- to late '70s ushered in the first commercially released samplers manufactured by Fairlight and Synclavier. Although highly advanced, these units were very expensive and thus simply out of reach for the average musician.

By the '80s, samplers had reached a price point where the average person could afford them. In 1987, Emu release the SP1200, a sampling drum machine, which was and still is regarded as one of the best instruments used in hip-hop production to date. Akai released its S1000 series sampler in 1988, which became the industry standard, with CD-quality resolution.

In the '90s, several manufacturers started production on sample-based instruments called workstations. These had samplers built within them, but also came preconfigured with a massive sound library.

By the late '90s, computer software engineers began working on developing software versions of samplers. In the last ten years, these software samplers have became extremely popular, as there are few limitations when compared to their hardware counterparts. Faster computers, ever higher amounts of RAM, and direct disk streaming have taken this concept to even new heights.

How a Sampler Works

Sampling involves recording a portion of audio. It may be a drum loop, or an individual tone, or even your washing machine on the spin cycle. Anything can be used as fodder for sound design when using a sampler.

Sample Editor

Most samplers include a built-in editor, which helps you prepare and add effects to your newly recorded sample.

Start and End

A common edit that is routinely performed is the removing of empty space before or after the sample. These are referred to respectively as the Start and End points of the sample.

Cropping

Cropping examines the samples' Start and End points and deletes any undesired information before or after the sample.

Loop

There may be times where you wish to extend the duration of the sample. This is achieved by setting loop points. Consider a loop to be like an additional Start and End point for the sample. When you trigger a sample, the original attack or transient is played, followed by the designated loop section, which is looped for as long at the trigger, or key, is held. Setting the release portion of the Amplifier envelope to a longer duration will cause the looped sound to continue after the release.

Cross-fade

This function creates smooth transitions between the start and end points of the loop cycle. Some samplers will also allow for cross-fading between multiple samples.

Fade-in / Fade-out

This introduces a fade-in at the beginning of the sample or a fade-out at the end of the sample.

Reverse

This reverses the audio waveform, which results in the sample's being played backward.

Normalize

This function increases the samples amplitude, or loudness, by finding the loudest point within the sample and increasing the overall sample to a designated level, such as 0 dB.

Key Zone

Once the sample has been edited and is ready to playback, it is loaded into a key zone. The key zone defines where the sample is placed on the keyboard. You may have a single key zone, the range of which could span the entire keyboard, or you may have several key zones, each being assigned to a single key on your keyboard. By default, a single sample is loaded into one key zone the range of which covers the entire span of the keyboard. As you play higher or lower on your MIDI controller keyboard, the pitch of the sample is either increased or decreased.

Key Map
A key map is a collection of several key zones.

Root Note
The root note sets where the sample plays back at its original pitch.

Multisampling
Multisampling is the process of using several samples within a key map to create a realistic-sounding instrument that seems to be playing in different octaves.

Consider sampling a vocalist singing the phrase, "Love is all you need," at middle C. If you were to playback the sample single octave above the original pitch, your singer would sound like a Chipmunk. And if you were to play the sample one octave lower, the voice would likely sound demonic.

Figure 3.1

To achieve realism across the entire range of your keyboard, you would need to record multiple samples at different pitches and map them accordingly.

In Fig. 3.1, you see the key map of a Farfisa organ. The current selected key zone shows a range from A#1 to D#2, with the root note set at C2. Also notice that the name of the sample reflects what key the original sample was recorded in. In this case, as is displayed, it's C2.

Fig. 3.2 shows the same key map of the Farfisa organ with the next key zone selected. Notice that the range is set from E2 to A2, with the root note set at F#2. This key zone starts where the previous key zone stops.

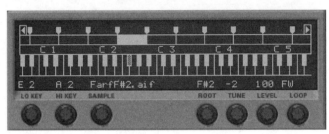

Figure 3.2

Sampling in Reason
Sampling in Reason is fairly straightforward. The process can be done using the Song Sample tab in the Tool window or by sampling directly into certain instruments, such as the NN-19, NN-XT, ReDrum, and/or Kong Drum Designer.

Preparing to Sample
You'll need to review a few settings and the available options before diving into the actual process.

Setting Up the Recording Formats
Whenever you are recording into Reason, the software will examine your audio preferences to determine the quality. Reason will record files in .WAV format at various bit depth and sample rate resolutions. The software will provide any conversions necessary to keep playback consistent and smooth.

The lowest settings that I recommend using are a sample rate of 44.1 KHz and a bit depth of 16 bits. This is the standard for CD-quality sound.

Setting Your Inputs
Whatever kind of sound you are sampling will determine how the signals are routed to the Sampling Input.

Figure 3.3

In Fig. 3.3, Audio Inputs 1 and 2 are routed to the Sampling Input on the Hardware Interface. This is the default wiring and is set up to record samples from the microphone or line inputs connected to your physical audio interface.

It is possible to record an instruments output, which allows for some creative sound design with resampling capabilities.

Sampling into the Song Sample Tool Window
In this tutorial, let's sample a drum loop from the ReDrum drum machine. I've gone ahead and programmed a four-bar drum loop. Feel free to create your own loop and follow along.

Routing the ReDrum
By default, when you created the ReDrum, it was automatically cabled to the 14:2 mixer. You can either route the output of the ReDrum direct to the Sampler inputs or, if you're planning on sampling multiple instruments and effects, you can use an Aux send on the mixer.

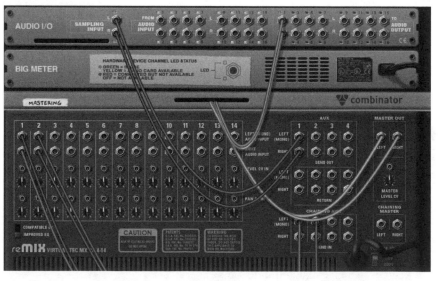

Figure 3.4

In this case, I've decided to use Aux 1 to route the signal to the Sampler inputs. This way Aux 1 can route any additional instruments I wish to sample without needing additional cabling.

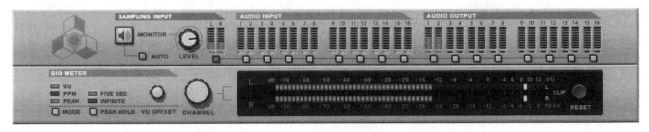

Figure 3.5

Make sure the Big Meter is engaged and the focus is positioned on the Sampler input, which is indicated by the red LED just below vertical meters on the Hardware Interface.

With the ReDrum playing, increase the setting of the Aux 1 knob on the mixer channel with the connected ReDrum. The idea is to get a loud signal without clipping. If the clip indicator lights up, then try lowering the Aux send.

Please note that if you engage the Monitor button, you'll hear both the original ReDrum and the signal coming through the Sampler input. This is normal and will not affect the quality of your sample.

Open the Song Sample Tab from the Tool Window

Once the Song Sample tab is open, you will find three sample folders: Assigned, Unassigned, and Self-Contained.

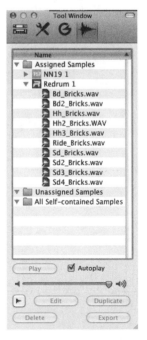

Figure 3.6

Assigned Samples

This folder contains any samples used by any instruments. In this case, you have an NN-19 and the ReDrum. The ReDrum folder unfolds to show the ten samples used in the kit.

Unassigned Samples

This folder contains any samples that have not yet been assigned to an instrument. This may be samples included in the Factory Sound Bank or samples that have been recorded.

Self-Contained Samples

This folder contains any samples you've recorded. All self-contained samples are saved within the Reason song. This helps with the file maintenance, because you never have to worry about samples used in a particular song getting lost or misplaced.

Sampling the ReDrum

Figure 3.7

As the levels are already set, let's proceed with the recording of your drum loop.

With the ReDrum stopped, hit the Start Sampling button on the Song Samples tab of the floating Tool window (see Fig. 3.7).

Once the Sample Record window is open and recording, click the Run button on the ReDrum.

Figure 3.8

You will now see the waveform displayed in the Recording window. Once the entire drum loop has played through once, click the Stop button on the Song Sample window transport.

Fig. 3.9 displays the newly recorded sample, named Sample 1, in both the unused and self-contained folders.

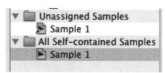

Figure 3.9

Notice the icon in the unused folder has a small arrow in the bottom left. This indicates that it has been designated as an alias file, which points to somewhere else in the system. In this case, the alias is pointing to the self-contained Sample 1 file.

If you were to look at any sample in the assigned sample folder, you would find that all of these samples are alias files with their actual files permanently located within the Reason Factory Sound Bank. This measure prevents you from mistakenly deleting or modifying any sample content within the factory settings. Any editing of samples taken from the Factory Sound folder automatically re-creates a new file, so as to not modify the original data.

Edit Samples

Select Sample 1 and click the Edit button at the bottom of the Song Sample transport window.

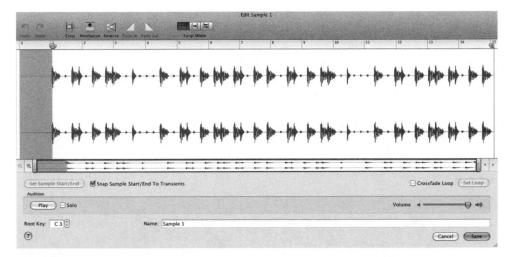

Figure 3.10

- The first thing you'll want to do is set the Start and End times and the loop sample to be used for your drum loop.
- Select the Forward Loop setting, which is the center button located under Loop Mode.

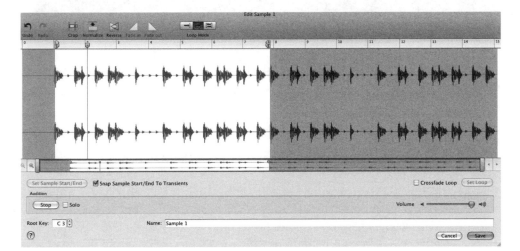

Figure 3.11

- Next, select the Start/End times to Transient option.
- Click the Play button and move the End time so that it will complete one full loop.

- Finally, click the Crop button to remove the recording data left outside the designated Start/End time.

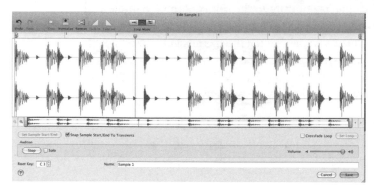

Figure 3.12

- Click the Normalize button to increase the level of the sample.
- Let's also change the name of the sample from Sample 1 to Drum Loop 1.
- The final step is to click the Save button to exit out of Edit mode.

NN-19 Digital Sampler

The NN-19 is a fantastic instrument. Reason ships with a comprehensive library of ready-made presets for the NN-19.

Figure 3.13

This instrument is also ideal for use in loading or recording your own sounds. It can be loaded with up to 127 samples, one for every key on the keyboard, and the key zones do not overlap.

Loading Patches

The presets for the NN-19 are loaded just as any other instrument in Reason by using the Browse Patch function.

I chose the Raw_MM_Sqr1 patch found in the Synth Raw Elements folder within the NN-19 Sampler patches.

This particular patch has two samples loaded into two key zones.

Selecting the Select Zone via MIDI button allows you to watch the zone automatically update as you play up the keyboard. You will learn how to create a custom patch in a later section.

Keyboard Window

The keyboard window displays the entire currently used key map. In this case, there are two distinct key zones. Each key zone displays settings across the bottom that define its programming.

Figure 3.14

Lo Key

The Lo key establishes the lowest note of the key zone. Turn the knob to adjust the key.

Hi Key

The Hi key establishes the highest note of the key zone. Turn the knob to adjust the key.

Select Sample

Select Sample shows what sample is currently loaded into the key zone. Turn the knob to scroll through any loaded samples.

Root

The Root knob establishes the root note by designating a key on the MIDI controller keyboard to play back the sample at its original pitch.

Tune

The Tune knob allows for control over the tuning or pitch of the sample. This gives a range of –50 to +50 cents.

Level

The Level control adjusts the volume of the sample.

Loop

The Loop knob selects whether the current sample will loop. The three modes available are Off, Forward, and Forward/Backward.

Synth Parameters

The synth parameters are used to shape and modulate the sounds produced by the sample. The original sample is left intact while all processing is made to the playback of the samples.

Osc

The Oscillator section controls the pitch of samples. All controls are global and affect all the samples within the patch.

Sample Start

This knob causes the sample to begin at a later point. This is helpful if you're using custom samples that have a bit of air at the beginning or if you want to modify how the sample starts.

Figure 3.15

Oct

The Octave knob increases or decreases the pitch range twelve semitones at a time.

Semi

The Semitone knob changes the pitch up to twelve semitones.

Fine

Fine, also known as cents, allows you to precisely change the pitch between semitones. There are 100 cents per semitone.

Env Amt

The Envelope Amount controls how much effect the Filter envelope will have on the pitch of the instrument. This is great for shaping the pitch over time.

Kbd Track

This button, when engaged, will allow the sample to change pitch according to what keys are pressed on your MIDI controller keyboard. Disengaging this parameter will cause the sample to play from its designated root note anywhere on the keyboard. This is useful for nonpitched samples such as drums, where it isn't ideal for the pitch to alter.

Filter

The NN-19 is equipped with a multimode filter with cutoff and resonance. It contains the same filter types found on the Subtractor: Notch, HP 12, BP 12, LP 12, and LP 24.

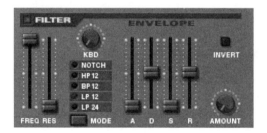

Figure 3.16

KBD

The Keyboard knob controls how the filter tracks across the keyboard. When turned fully clockwise, the filter cutoff will increase as you play up the keyboard.

Filter Envelope

The Filter envelope allows you to shape the filter over time.

Amp

The Amplifier section controls the level of the instrument. There is a dedicated Level control and a dedicated Amp envelope.

Figure 3.17

LFO

The LFO section contains the usual assortment of waveforms for use as a modulation source.

Figure 3.18

The Rate knob controls the frequency or speed of the LFO. It has a Sync button, which forces the LFO to work in musical increments, such as eighth or sixteenth notes.

The amount controls how much LFO is sent to the set destination, with options including the Oscillator, Filter, and Pan.

Play Parameters

The Play parameters are designed to help with expression by controlling or modifying incoming MIDI messages.

Figure 3.19

Portamento

This knob controls the glide function. Instead of notes changing instantaneously to the next note or pitch, the sound instead glides into the new pitch.

Polyphony

This parameter controls the number of voices the sampler will play at once. A Polyphony setting of 1 is essentially the same as a monophonic setting.

Spread

This dynamically changes the panning of voices. The Spread knob controls how much spreading occurs.

Key

Key spreads the sounds across the stereo field. Lower notes on the keyboard appear to the left in the stereo field. As you play higher, the stereo field tracks across the keyboard with higher notes appearing in the right side of the stereo field.

Key 2

Key 2 spreads the pan position from left to right in eight steps as each consecutive higher note is played on the keyboard. Once eight steps have been reached, the cycle is repeated.

Jump

Jump will alternate between the left and right stereo fields with every note played.

Figure 3.20

Legato

This style of playing, triggering a new note without releasing the previous note, will not trigger a new envelope.

Retrigger

This mode forces the envelopes to retrigger, regardless of your playing style.

Controller

This parameter sets up which incoming MIDI controller will have control over the Filter Frequency, LFO, and Amplifer amounts. The MIDI controllers that the NN-19 will respond to include Aftertouch, Expression Pedal, and Breath Control.

Figure 3.21

Pitch Bend

This setting affects the range of the Pitch Bend. The range can be set up to twenty-four semitones plus or minus, to cover a total of four octaves.

Mod Wheel

The Modulation wheel can be programmed to control Filter Frequency, Filter Resonance, Filter Envelope Decay, Amplifier, and LFO amounts. All controls can be set to positive or negative and can all be controlled simultaneously.

Velocity

This setting controls what parameters will respond to incoming velocity messages. The available parameters include Filter Envelope amount, Filter Envelope Decay, Amplifier Level, Amplifier Envelope Attack, and Sample Start.

Creating Custom Patches

Figure 3.22

With the NN-19 selected, click Initialize Patch from the Edit menu.

Next, click the Browse Sample button, located above the keyboard display.

From the Browse Sample window, select MM_Saw_C1 and MM_Saw_C3 from the MiniMoog Samples folder found in the Synth Raw Elements folder located in the NN-19 Sampler Patches.

Keyboard Display

When initializing a patch, only one key zone is created, which spans the entire range of the keyboard. The solid light blue line above the keyboard denotes this.

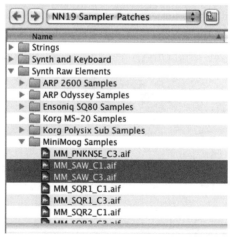

Figure 3.23

Figure 3.24

The first sample you selected from the browser is automatically selected; regardless of how many samples you've loaded. In this case, you've loaded a total of two samples.

If you turn the Sample knob, you can switch between the two loaded samples.

To play both samples, you need to create a new key zone, which is done by selecting Split Key Zone from the Edit menu.

Another useful function found in the Edit menu is the Automap Samples function. This works especially well if the sample contains pitch information. Most samples can contain pitch data, which the NN-19 can read and assign to the appropriate key zone and root note. The C1 and C3 parts of the title let you know that these samples contain this information.

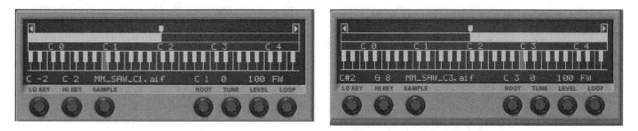

Figure 3.25

In Fig. 3.25, you see the Keyboard window with both key zones showing.

The key zone on the left has its Lo key and Hi key set to C–2 to C2, respectively. The sample is set to MM_Saw_C1.aif. The root note is set to C1 and the loop mode is set to Forward. Note the correlation between the C1 in the name of the sample with the root note.

The key zone on the right has its Lo key and Hi key set to C#2 and G8, respectively. The sample is set to MM_Saw_C3.aif. The root note is set to C3. Again, note the correlation between the C3 in the sample name and the root note.

Sampling into the NN-19

Let's take a look at how to sample directly into the NN-19 sampler.

First, initialize the instrument by selecting the Initialize Patch function found in the Edit menu.

Once it's initialized, make sure your connections are set up properly. Earlier in this chapter, you sampled the ReDrum via an aux send on the mixer. This time you're going to sample via a line input, so you'll need to route Audio Inputs 1 and 2 to the Sampling Inputs and check the levels.

Once you've got your levels set, click on the Sample button and play the proposed sample.

Figure 3.26

Figure 3.27

The now familiar Recording window opens and displays the recorded waveform. Press the Stop button to assign a key zone for the sample that spans the entire keyboard.

Next, let's add another sample.

You'll need to create a new key zone by selecting Split Key Zone from the Edit menu. You'll notice a new key zone has been created with "no sample" loaded.

Follow the same procedure for recording a sample. You can repeat this process as many times as you like. Also remember that the samples can be edited using the Song Sample tab of the Tool window.

NN-XT

The NN-XT was released as the successor to the NN-19, but was never intended to replace it. Both samplers feature the same core structure, which allows for assigning samples to key zones with multiple key zones available per patch. Both have similar synth parameters used to shape and modulate the sounds, but the NN-XT takes things to the next level with the added abilities to program layers and enable velocity-controlled switching and cross-fades.

Figure 3.28

The setup is simple yet has such added features as Duplicate and Copy parameters from a key zone, Auto-zone Mapping, and Pitch Detection for assigning root notes.

Main Panel

In Fig. 3.28, you see the main panel featuring global control over the Filter and Amp envelope parameters, as well as the Decay for the Modulation envelope and Master Volume.

The familiar Pitch and Mod wheels are found with an additional X wheel, which generates Aftertouch, Expression, or Breath Control messages. This feature provides added sound shaping control, in case your keyboard controller isn't capable of transmitting these messages.

Remote Editor

At the bottom of the main panel, the NN-XT offers the Remote editor. Fig. 3.29 shows the unfolded Remote editor with the CrickleWood patch selected from the Synth Lead folder for the NN-XT sampler.

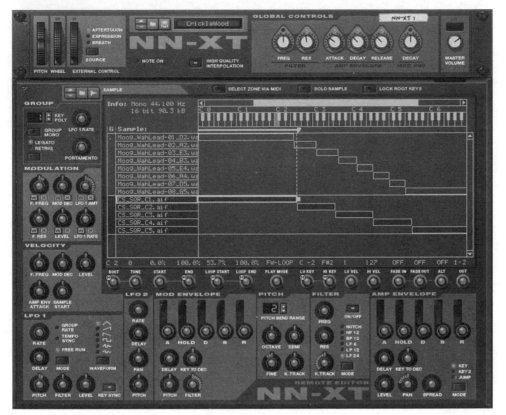

Figure 3.29

The main section of the editor is the Key Map display, which shows the loaded samples and key zones grouped together. In this particular patch, you see two zone groups layered together in the same key map, which will result in both sounds playing together as one.

Just below the Key Map is the Sample parameter bar, which gives you independent control over settings for each key zone or sample.

Group and synth parameters are located on the left and bottom of the editor.

Key Map Display

The Key Map display is very much like the one featured in the NN-19, but with some additional enhancements and features.

The upper left of the window shows the Info bar, which gives a detailed breakdown of the currently selected sample. The info shown contains the Mono or Stereo, Sample Rate, Bit Depth, and Size settings.

The keyboard display is situated on the right side. The solid light blue bar at the top is the scroll bar, which permits a view of the entire keyboard range by clicking and dragging the scroll bar left to right.

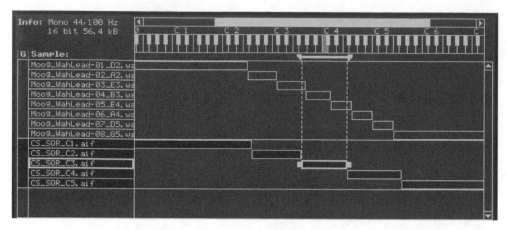

Figure 3.30

The left column, just below the Info bar, displays the Sample list. Fig. 3.30 shows the CS_SQR group, which is denoted by the vertical running bar situated next to the collected list of samples. Clicking on this vertical group bar selects all samples and key zones in the designated group.

To the right of the sample list column are several horizontal bars, indicating the range for each key zone in which individual samples are loaded.

The centered sample has an Edit Focus, consisting of light blue handles attached to either side of the key zone. You'll also see dotted lines running up toward the Tab bar. By selecting either the handles or the Tab bar, you can adjust the key zone's Hi and Lo parameters. Remember that it is possible to select and edit multiple key zones at once.

Sample Parameters

The Sample parameter section allows detailed control over each sample or sample grouping.

Figure 3.31

The M on some parameters denotes the particular samples within the group that have different settings.

Root

This control determines at what note the sample will play back at its original pitch.

Tune

This control allows for fine-tuning of the sample in Cents. There are 100 cents per semitone, with the designate control range of –50 to +50.

Start

This control determines the start time of the sample.

End

This control determines the end time of the sample.

Loop Start

This control determines the loop start point within the sample.

Loop End

This control determines the loop end point within the sample.

Play Mode

This control determines the loop mode.

FW

This loop mode plays the sample forward. The sample will play through once and then stop.

FW-Loop

This loop mode also plays the sample forward, but in this case, the sample will loop continually between the loop's start and end times. This loop will continue to play even after the key is released.

FW-BW

This loop mode plays the sample forward, but once the sample reaches the loop's end point, it plays backward to the loop's start point and then repeats the cycle continually.

FW-SUS

This loop functions like FW-Loop, only once the key is released, the sample plays through the rest of the sample outside the designated loop's end point. This allows samples to retain their natural decay.

BW

This loop play mode plays through once, only in reverse.

Lo Key

This control determines the lowest key in a key zone.

Hi Key

This control determines the highest key in a key zone.

Lo Vel

This control determines the lowest velocity message the sample will trigger.

Hi Vel

This control determines the highest velocity message the sample will trigger.

Fade In

Used for velocity cross-fades, this control determines up to which velocity value will have a fade-in effect. Values above the Fade In level will play at full velocity.

Fade Out

Used for velocity fades and cross-fades, this control determines what setting the velocity value will establish a fade-out effect. Values up to the designated Fade level play at full velocity. After this value is reached, the levels will then fade out.

Alt

This control, when enabled, will alternate through any number of specified samples. To use this function, set the key ranges to an exact or partial overlap. Select all the samples you wish to alternate, and enable Alt function so that each time the key is hit, it will randomly switch between selected samples.

Out

This control determines the output for a group or sample. There are sixteen outputs arranged in stereo pairs. To gain access to sixteen individual outputs, select two samples and route them to a stereo pair output. Then, hard pan each sample and route each output to its own channel on the mixer.

Group Parameters

Group parameters affect all samples assigned to a group. They typically affect the style in which the samples are played.

Figure 3.32

Key Poly

This parameter affects the number of keys that can be pressed. The range is 1 to 99, with a setting of 1 equal to monophonic playback.

Group Mono

This parameter overrides the Key Poly setting and allows only one sample in the group to be triggered at a time. However, if the Key Poly is set to any value over 1, then that particular sample may be retriggered polyphonically. It's only when switching between two or more samples that the mono function will take effect.

Legato/Retrig

Legato is a playing style that prevents the envelopes of a new sound from being triggered when you are holding down the key of a previous note. For example, with this setting engaged, play and hold one key on your keyboard and trigger a second note without releasing the first note. The pitch of the note will change, but the envelopes will not be triggered.

LFO 1 Rate

This is a group override that takes precedence over the LFO 1 settings in the Synth Parameter section.

Portamento

This function will cause notes to glide between note pitches, as opposed to jumping instantly to the next pitch value.

Synth Parameters

The NN-XT has the all the typical synth parameters used for sound shaping and modulation.

Modulation

The Modulation section features control parameters for Filter Frequency, Filter Resonance, Modulation Envelope Decay, Level, LFO 1 Amount, and LFO 1 Rate.

Figure 3.33

Each control is assigned to either the Modulation wheel (W) or External control (X). Each parameter can be set to positive or negative, affording a wide variety of tone shaping control, all simultaneously.

Velocity

The Velocity section offers control over the Filter Frequency, Modulation Envelope Decay, Level, Amplifier Envelope Attack, and Sample Start settings.

Figure 3.34

LFO 1

LFO 1 offers the same waveform shapes as any other synthesizer in Reason. The destinations available are set as Pitch, Filter, and Level.

Figure 3.35

The rate knob offers settings for Group Rate, Tempo Sync, and Free Run.

It also features a Delay knob, which will delay the onset of the LFO 1 en route to its destination.

A Key Sync feature is also available, in which the LFO will retrigger with each new note.

Figure 3.36

LFO 2

LFO 2 has a set triangle waveform with destinations for Pan and Pitch.

The Rate control is set to free run.

It also offers a delay, which, just as with LFO 1, will delay the onset of the LFO en route to its destination.

Mod Envelope

The Modulation envelope offers the standard ADSR, with a Hold function that grabs the Decay portion for a set time before continuing on to Sustain.

Figure 3.37

It offers destinations to Pitch and Filter Frequency.

The Delay knob will delay the onset of the envelope to its destination.

It also offers Key to Decay, which forces the Decay portion of the envelope to track across the keyboard. With a positive setting, the Decay will increase as you play higher up the keyboard.

Pitch

The pitch section offers control for the Pitch Bend settings, with a range –24 to +24 octaves.

Figure 3.38

There are dedicated tune controls for Octave, Semitone, and Fine (Cents).

It also offers Key Track that, when turned fully counterclockwise, will cause the pitch to be constant. Turning the knob fully clockwise will increase the pitch by one octave.

Filter

The NN-XT multimode filter offers a variety of filter types, including Notch, HP 12, BP 12, LP 6, LP 12, and LP 24.

The filter controls include Frequency Cutoff and Resonance, as well as Key Track, which, when enabled, will cause the Frequency to follow the keys on the keyboard. A positive setting will result in the Filter Frequency opening up as you play higher notes on the keyboard.

Figure 3.39

Amp Envelope

The Amplifier envelope offers the same controls as the Modulation envelope, including ADSR with the Hold function previously described.

There are also a Delay function and a Keyboard to Decay function, as described in the Modulation Env section.

Figure 3.40

In addition, the Amp envelope offers a dedicated Level control and a comprehensive Pan section.

The Pan section has controls for spread with mode settings for Key, Key 2, and Jump.

Key

This control causes the sound to pan from left to right, based on where you play on the keyboard. Playing in lower octaves will pan the sound to the left, whereas playing higher will cause panning to the right.

Key 2

This will cause the sound to pan from left to right in an eight-note cycle.

Jump

This control causes the sound to alternate left and right with each key pressed.

Velocity Switching

Now let's examine a preset that offers velocity switching.

Click the Browse Patch button on the main interface and select Brush Kit from the Drums and Percussion folder.

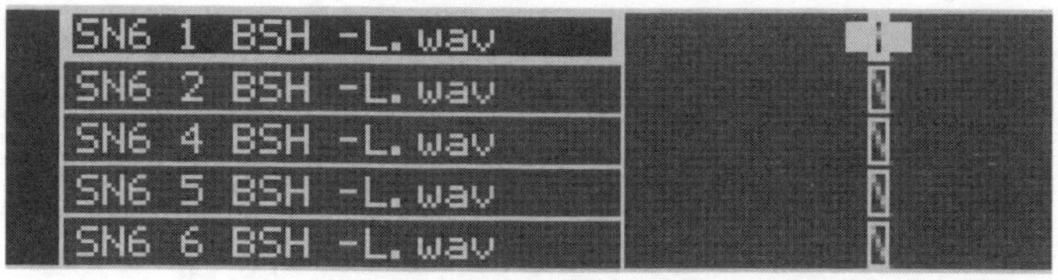

Figure 3.41

Click the Select Zone via MIDI button at the top of the editor.

Next, play D1 on your MIDI controller keyboard. Notice how each strike of differing velocities will trigger a one of six different snare samples. This adds an element of realism because a genuine snare drum will sound different when struck at different velocities. Some drum sample libraries offer over fifty levels of velocity switching, each with a different sample assigned to it.

Creating a Custom Patch

Let's take a look at how to create a custom patch.

Programming Custom High Hats

- Start by initializing the NN-XT, by selecting Initialize Patch from the Edit menu.
- Next, use the Browse Sample button to select a high hat sound. I have selected Hat3-03 from the Click House Dub Samples folder, found in NN-XT Sample Patches > Drums and Percussion > Drums and Kits.
- Once loaded, select Automap Chromatically from the Edit menu. This will set the key range and root note to C1.
- Next, with the sample selected, click Duplicate Zones from the Edit menu. Do this a second time to create three duplicates of your high hat.
- Next, select Solo Sample at the top of the Remote editor. This enables you to hear only the selected sample.

Figure 3.42

- Now, change the Amp Env to reflect the settings shown in Fig. 3.42. The Decay setting is set to 60 ms. Then repeat this procedure for all three samples.
- On each sample, first vary the filter cutoff and resonance slightly and then adjust the pitch plus or minus four semitones.
- Then, select the group of samples and engage the Alt function.
- Last, turn off the Solo Sample function and play your high hat. You will notice that with each hit of the key, the samples triggered will alternate to allow for a different sample to play each time.

Be sure to save your work, because you may utilize this sound again in the Advanced Sequencing chapter.

Chapter 4
REASON DRUM AND PERCUSSION INSTRUMENTS

Dr. OctoRex

The Dr. OctoRex Loop Player is a loop playback device that uses Rex files as content. Rex files are loops that have been processed by Recycle, a utility program created by Propellerhead. This program analyzes the loops and breaks them up into slices based on the transient of each sound within the loop. The Recycled file also generates a MIDI file that allows the loop to be played as originally produced. A huge benefit of using this technology is that you can play virtually any loop at any tempo without affecting the pitch.

Before the advent of Recycle, the task of manually slicing loops and programming MIDI sequences was a tedious, time-consuming task, usually taking several hours to process a single loop. Recycle, however, does all the work for you instantaneously.

If you are creating your own loops and wish to use them as Recycled files, then purchasing Recycle is a must. Do note however, that Reason ships with a stocked library of Rex files. The available loops range from drum and percussion loops to instrument and FX, or effect, loops.

Dr. OctoRex Instrument Panel

The main interface at the top of the device as shown contains the familiar Pitch Bend and Mod wheel, eight-loop slot selector buttons, Master Volume, and Global Transpose settings.

Figure 4.1

Clicking the Run button (with enable loop playback engaged) will cause the loop to start playing. This function is completely independent of the transport control.

The current default preset is Acoustic Drums—College 130. Selecting any of the loop slots will switch between variations on the Acoustic Drum loops.

Global Transpose

This changes the pitch globally by semitones. The parameter settings from +12 to –12 provide a total range of two full octaves.

Trig Next Loop

This sets the time division at which a new loop will start. The default setting of Bar waits for the currently playing loop to reach the end of a bar, before triggering the new one. This proves to be a handy function for keeping everything in time.

Show Programmer

Once the programmer is unfolded, you will find the loop slot selection and Slice editor positioned to the left and the familiar synth parameter controls located to the right.

Select Loop and Load Slot

The eight buttons in the programmer coincide with the main loop selector at the top of the instrument panel. Each slot holds an individual loop. Selecting the Loop Browser button imports a new Rex files into the selected slot.

Copy Loop to Track

Copy Loop to Track generates a MIDI file and places it on the Dr. OctoRex track in the Sequencer window.

Slice Editor

Below the loop slots is the Slice editor. A red line placed at the beginning of each transient denotes each slice. You may select a slice by either clicking on it or using a MIDI note. (Make sure the Select Slice by MIDI setting is activated.)

Each slice has independent control over Pitch, Pan, Level, Decay, Reverse, Filter Frequency, Alternate Group, and Output.

There are also Loop Transpose and Loop Level settings that can affect the currently selected loop in the Loop editor.

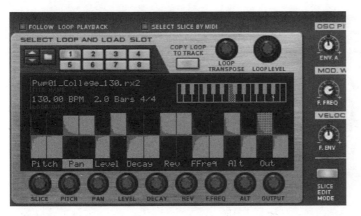

Figure 4.2

Selecting the Slice Edit Mode button, shown in the lower right corner of Fig. 4.2, allows for fast programming of slices by drawing in desired values with the Pencil tool.

Here, notice how I have panned each drum hit opposite the other.

Alternate Outputs

By using Tab to select to the back of the device, note that the Dr. OctoRex has four stereo outputs in addition to the main output.

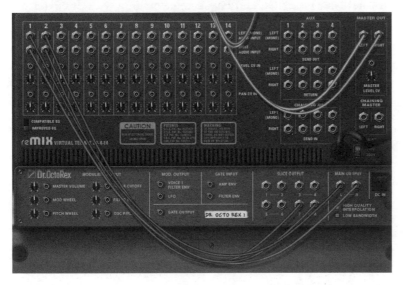

Figure 4.3

Next, cable Outputs 7 and 8 into mixer Channel 2.

Tab to the front of the interface and select Slot 2 on the main interface.

Using Slice Edit Mode, select the Out setting on the Slice editor.

Route every snare hit to Out 7–8. Select Run and note how the snare is now routed to a separate channel on the mixer. This provides for creative processing, such as adding reverb or delay to just the snare hits alone, among other techniques.

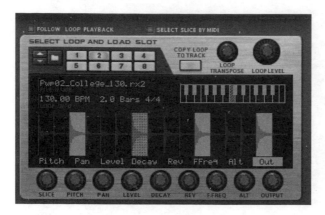

Figure 4.4

Synth Parameters

The synth parameters of the Dr. OctoRex are global and will affect the instrument as a whole.

There are dedicated control sections for Osc Pitch, Modulation wheel assignment, Velocity, Multimode Filter, LFO, and its dedicated Filter and Amp envelopes.

LFO Effects

The LFO has the destinations Osc, Filter, and Pan. Experimenting with these during production can really breathe new life into a static drum loop.

Envelopes

Increasing the attack of either envelope can lead to pseudo-backward effects.

ReDrum Drum Computer

The ReDrum Drum computer's design is based on the vintage drum machines released in the early '80s by Roland. Since their release, the TR-808 and TR-909 models were targeted toward professional musicians. Unfortunately, however, they sounded completely unrealistic when compared to a standard acoustic kit and the line was, at last, discontinued.

In spite of this, with the emergence of modern electronic music as a genre throughout the '80s, these drum machines eventually became a staple of the sound. The TR-909 became the quintessential sound associated with house music, while the TR-808 was responsible for spawning the sounds of early hip-hop and Miami bass.

Still highly coveted today, these unique machines still have a huge following with many producers, some of whom are willing to pay considerably more than the units originally sold for.

Luckily for producers like us, Propellerhead developed a software program known as ReBirth in 1996. A precursor to Reason, ReBirth featured software emulations of both the TR-808 and TR-909.

When Reason was first released in 2000, it included another emulation component called the ReDrum Drum Computer. This sample-based drum machine came equipped with a sixty-four-step sequencer, which was also modeled after the early Roland machines.

The ReDrum instrument interface consists of three primary sections: the Global section, the Drum Sound parameter, and the Sequencer. Entire kits can be loaded or individual drum sounds into each of the instrument's ten channels.

Figure 4.5

Global Section

The Global section is where you can save and load kits via the Save Patch and Browse Patch buttons.

Figure 4.6

High-Quality Interpolation

When engaged, this will cause an advanced algorithm to interpolate samples, thereby creating in higher-quality results. This function, however, requires more processing power and it is recommended for use only when deemed necessary. The best way to determine this need is to audition the parameter within the context of other tracks.

Exclusive 8 and 9

This option, when engaged, forces each channel to behave monophonically. For example, if Channel 8 is triggered, followed by Channel 9, Channel 9 will cut off the sound of Channel 8, rendering it exclusive to Channel 9.

Master Volume

This knob, located on the upper left side of the interface, controls the overall level of the main outputs.

Drum Sound Parameters

Common Drum Parameters

The Drum Sound parameters of each channel share some commonality.

Figure 4.7

Located in order from the top are the Mute, Solo, and Play buttons. Below is the name of the sample being used, loaded onto the specific track with the sample browse functions available underneath.

To the right of the Browse Sample button is a dedicated Sample button. This allows for the recording of samples directly into the interface. Refer to chapter 3 for the full procedure regarding recording samples.

S1 and S2, Stereo, and Pan Controls

S1 and S2

Send 1 and Send 2, when connected to the mixer, route their respective signals to the Channel Aux input, allowing any channel direct access to effects connected to the mixer.

Figure 4.8

Stereo Sample

When illuminated, the two cojoined circles displayed between S1 and S2 indicate the currently located sample is set to stereo.

Pan

This knob controls the left and/or right balance of the sound within the stereo field.

Level, Length, and Decay

Figure 4.9

Level

The Level knob controls the amplitude of individual sample. There's also a Velocity knob that controls how the level responds to velocity messages.

Length

This knob controls the length of the sample. When positioned to the right, the sample is played in its entirety, but when positioned to the left, the sample is shortened.

Decay

Figure 4.10

The Decay switch acts as an envelope and controls how the sample ends. The triangle shape will produce a natural-sounding decay, whereas the square creates an abrupt cutoff.

Pitch, Tone, and Sample Start

The following controls will vary, depending on which channel is being utilized.

Channels 1, 2, and 10

Pitch

This knob controls the pitch of the sample, plus or minus one octave. When centered, the LED is not illuminated and the sample is played at that sample's original pitch. Moving this knob to the right raises the pitch, whereas moving it to the left lowers the pitch.

Tone

Figure 4.11

This knob controls the brightness of the sound. When centered, the sound is unaffected, but moving it to the right increases the brightness, whereas moving it to the left decreases it.

The Velocity knob controls how the Tone knob reacts to the note velocity.

Channels 3, 4, 5, 8, and 9

Pitch

Control is the same as for Channels 1, 2, and 10.

Start

This knob controls the start of the sample. The default setting is at the far left and plays the sample from its beginning. Moving the knob to the right, shifts the start time, thereby cutting off the sample start. This can be a useful function for removing dead space from a sample. Likewise, it can also be used to soften the attack.

The velocity knob controls how the sample start reacts to incoming note velocity.

Channels 6 and 7

Pitch with Bend

These channels offer pitch control with the ability to bend the pitch up or down, relative to the pitch setting.

Figure 4.12

The Rate knob controls how quickly the bend occurs.

The Velocity knob controls how the pitch/bend reacts to incoming note velocity.

The Sequencer

The sequencer features four banks, each consisting of eight patterns, for a total of thirty-two patterns per instrument.

Each sequence can have up to sixty-four steps with different resolution setting for each pattern.

Figure 4.13

To program the sequencer, click a Select button at the bottom of the Drum Parameter window. This notifies the sequencer that this is the particular sound you wish to sequence.

Next, click on a Step button wherever you wish to hear the desired sound.

Sequence Programming

Let's re-create the steps involved in programming a simple house pattern.

House Pattern

- First, select House Kit 7 from the Patch Browser.

Figure 4.14

- Next, click the Run button to activate the sequencer. The red LED will begin to cycle. Maintain the resolution at the default setting of a sixteenth note. This will establish a one-bar pattern.

Figure 4.15

- Now, select Channel 1. This channel is typically assigned to a kick drum sound.

Figure 4.16

- Select Steps 1, 5, 9, and 13. This will set up a quarter-note kick, which is a familiar pattern widely utilized in house and techno music.

- Next, select Channel 9, which is set to an open high-hat sound.
- Then select Steps 3, 7, 11, and 15.
- The open high hat in this particular preset has a very short length set. By changing this setting to 63, you will be able to hear more of the sample.
- Last, select Channel 2, which is a handclap sample, and click Steps 5 and 13.
- Congratulations! You've just created a simple house beat.

Figure 4.17

- Now, let's change the number for steps from 16 to 32 and produce some variations to your house pattern.

Figure 4.18

- To program Steps 17 through 32, first move the Edit Steps switch to be between 17 and 32.
- Follow the same programming you did previously for Steps 1 though 16.
- This should result in a two-bar sequence that sounds exactly the same.
- Next, between Steps 1 and 16, add a kick to Step 16.
- Then, between Steps 17 and 32, add a kick to Step 15.

Copy Pattern

- Click on the Pattern 1 button and use the Copy command (Control + C for PC, Command + C for Mac) to copy.
- Next, select Pattern 2 and use the Paste command (Control + V for PC, Command + C for Mac) to paste.
- Select Channel 8, a tambourine sample, and then click and drag from Step 1 through 16. This method is a very quick and effective way of adding a sixteenth-note pattern to your sequence without having to select each individual step. This method is also useful for removing sounds from a pattern.
- Do this for both sections 1 to 16 and 17 to 32.

Note how the sixteenth-note tambourine pattern sounds very mechanical. A great way to modify this to create some rhythmic variation to alter the dynamics of every other note, as described next.

Figure 4.19

Move the Dynamic switch setting to Soft.

Figure 4.20

Click on every even-numbered step in the sequence. This will create some dynamic variation, thereby adding a little more feeling into the sequence.

Shuffle

Adding a shuffle to a pattern changes the rhythmic timing by moving every even-numbered step a little closer to the odd-numbered steps.

Figure 4.21

To do this, first engage the Shuffle button on the ReDrum interface. Immediately, you should hear the pattern alter slightly, with more of a swing feel to the rhythm.

Figure 4.22

Next, click the ReGroove Mixer button located on the bottom right of the Transport.

Figure 4.23

On the bottom left side of the ReGroove Mixer, you find the Global Shuffle knob. This will adjust the overall shuffle of any device capable of the shuffle function, including the Matrix Pattern Sequencer and the RPG-8 Arpeggiator.

The parameters range from 50 to 75 percent, with 50 percent providing no effect.

A setting of 66 percent to this will create a perfect sixteenth-note triplet.

Using the ReDrum as a Sound Module

Another method of using the ReDrum is to bypass the sequencer and use it as a sound module, triggered by MIDI notes from your MIDI controller.

Triggering Sounds

Octave C1 triggers individual notes. This enables usage of a MIDI controller to play and record sounds into the Reason sequencer.

Triggering Mutes

Octave C2 acts as a momentary mute on each drum sound and allows you to play the mutes in a musical way, as well as to record these effects into the Sequencer window.

Triggering Solos

Octave C3 acts a momentary solo of each drum sound and allows you to play the solos in a musical way, as well as to record these effects into the Sequencer window.

Kong Drum Designer

The Kong Drum Designer is a sixteen-part multitimbre instrument capable creating a variety of drum and percussion sounds.

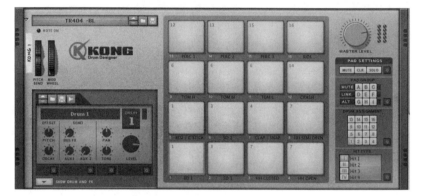

Figure 4.24

The interface contains sixteen pads, reminiscent of many hardware drum machines, most notably the Akai MPC series.

The three main sections of the Kong Drum Designer include the Pad section, the Drum control panel, and the Drum and FX programmer.

Triggering Pads

Pads are triggered by MIDI notes that can be easily played via any MIDI controller. Keyboard controllers are fine, but you may find, as I do, that a dedicated MIDI pad controller, such as the M-Audio Trigger Finger or the Akai MPD series, may offer a greater degree of control.

The C1 octave of your keyboard will trigger each sound in an ascending order (e.g., C1 triggers Pad 1, C#1 triggers Pad 2, etc.).

The C3 octave assigns each pad to every three keys on your keyboard. (e.g., C3, C#3, D3 to trigger Pad 1; D#3, E3, F3 to trigger Pad 2, etc.). This is useful for triggering the same pad in rapid-fire procession, which is normally a difficult task when only using one key on your MIDI controller.

The pads on the instrument interface itself are velocity sensitive. Clicking at the bottom of a pad generates a lower velocity, whereas triggering at the top of a pad triggers the maximum velocity. This can be a useful tool when you are programming sounds.

Loading Sounds

Located in the upper left corner is the Kit Patch selection, with the familiar Browse and Save Patch buttons. This will load entire kits with sounds allocated to each of the sixteen pads.

Figure 4.25

To load or save an individual drum patch, select a drum pad and use the Browse or Save Drum Patch section in the upper left corner of the Drum control panel. This section also offers direct sampling into each of the sixteen pads. Refer to chapter 3 for details on the process of recording samples.

Drums and FX

Before you start to create custom sounds, let's examine the signal flow of the Kong.

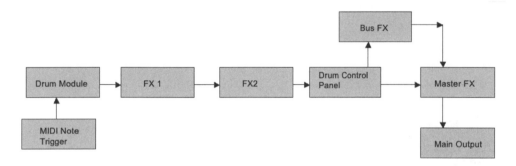

Figure 4.26

- A MIDI note triggers the Drum module.
- From the Drum module, the signal is passed through Insert FX 1 and Insert FX 2 serially.
- From FX 2, the signals passed into the Drum control panel.
- The Drum control panel then routes the signal to the Master FX section.
- The Drum control panel also offers an effects send to the Bus FX.
- The Bus FX output is routed through Master FX.
- The Master FX then routes the signal to the main outputs of the instrument.

There are variations whereby the output of the control panel maybe routed through the Bus FX or directly to the main or the individual outputs.

Drum Modules

The Drum modules available in the Kong Drum Designer are nothing short of spectacular. Each module offers unique ways to tailor your sound using samples, Rex files, physical modeling, and analog modeling. Depending on the type of module used, the Hit Type under Pad Settings will create a different effect. Let's first look at the available modules and then explore the Hit Type settings and how each affects performance.

NN-Nano Sampler

The NN-Nano Sampler takes its cues from the NN-XT sampler. It contains four hit slots, each with multiple layers.

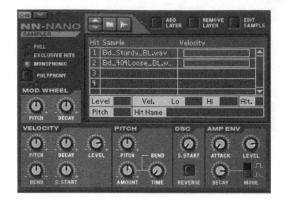

Figure 4.27

By loading multiple samples per hit slot, you can achieve sophisticated velocity switching between samples, a function that is quite useful for creating highly realistic sounds.

The Nano Sampler also features the usual assortment of sound-shaping capabilities, including parameters for precise control over Mod Wheel, Velocity, Pitch, and Osc and Amp envelope settings.

Nurse Rex Loop Player

The Nurse Rex Loop Player utilizes the same Rex player technology employed by the Dr. OctoRex Loop Player.

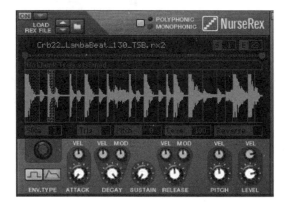

Figure 4.28

The Rex file will respond to various Hit Type settings, thereby providing some really creative ways to manipulate the loop, including Loop Trigger, Beat Juggling, and Individual Slice Triggering settings.

Also, included with the Nurse Rex are the usual synth controls, including velocity-controlled envelope stages (ADSR), as well as Pitch and Level control settings (also controlled by velocity).

Physical Bass Drum

Physical modeling synthesis provides unprecedented control over sound-shaping capabilities, which far exceeds the control of a sample playback device.

Figure 4.29

The Bass Drum physical modeling module offers control over the Beater, Drumhead, and Shell settings, each containing a variety of parameters.

Physical Snare Drum

The Physical Snare Drum offers control over the Shell and Snare, Drumhead, and Edge Tuning settings.

Figure 4.30

The assignment of different hit types gives you independent and precise control over Center, Position, and Edge.

Physical Tom Tom

The Physical Tom Tom drum offers control over the Drumstick, Drumhead, and Shell settings.

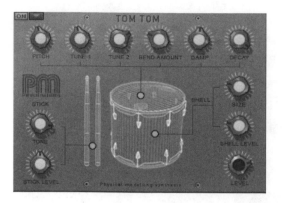

Figure 4.31

Synth Bass Drum

Analog modeling synthesis, much like physical modeling, affords an unprecedented control over sound-shaping capabilities, which far exceeds the control offered by a sample playback device.

The Bass Drum offers control over the Pitch, Tone, Click, and Envelope settings.

Figure 4.32

Synth High Hat

The Synth High Hat offers control over the Pitch, Decay, Level, Click, Tone, and Ring settings.

Hit Type control further offers four types of high-hat sounds: Closed, Semi-Closed, Semi-Open, and Open.

Figure 4.33

Synth Snare Drum

The Snare Drum module offers control over the Pitch, Decay, Level, Harmonics, and Noise settings.

Figure 4.34

Synth Tom Tom

The Synth Tom Tom module provides control of the Pitch, Click, Level, Decay, and Noise settings.

Figure 4.35

FX

The available effects include FX1, FX2, Bus FX, and Master FX.

Compressor

The compressor affords control over dynamics by rendering your louder sounds softer and your softer sounds louder.

Compressor settings include the Compression Amount, Attack, Release, and Makeup Gain.

Filter

This resonant multimode filter offers both standard cutoff and resonance control, with LP, BP, and HP settings. Also included is a MIDI-triggered envelope generator.

Figure 4.36   Figure 4.37

Figure 4.38

Overdrive / Resonator

Providing two effects in one, the Overdrive section offers a nice assortment of distortion, whereas the Resonator section is taken from the Body algorithms of the Scream Distortion processor.

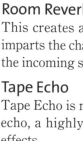

Figure 4.39

Parametric EQ

This is a single-band parametric equalizer with frequency control and gain. The Q parameter offers the ability to shape the bandwidth of the EQ, creating a wider band to the left and narrower band to the right.

Rattler

Set this device to add a snare rattle to any signal produced.

Figure 4.40

Ring Modulator

The ring modulator is based on a mathematical algorithm that combines the sum and difference of two distinct signals.

This particular unit has a built-in sine generator that works in tandem with the incoming signal to produce wild metallic like tones and effects.

Figure 4.43

Room Reverb

This creates a standard Room Reverb effect, which imparts the characteristics of variously sized rooms to the incoming signal.

Tape Echo

Tape Echo is modeled after the vintage Roland Space echo, a highly sought-after tape delay used for dub effects.

Figure 4.41

Transient Shaper

The Transient Shaper affords the ability to change the attack of any drum hit. This can be of great use when modifying drums to sit better in a mixer, without the use of EQ.

Figure 4.42

Figure 4.45

Support Generator Effects

These effects are only available with the FX 1 and FX 2, and are designed to add character and weight to an incoming signal. Additionally, the use of hit types allows for more precise control over when the device will generate sounds.

Figure 4.44

Noise Generator

This adds noise to the incoming signal. It also offers Envelope control with dedicated resonance, sweep, and click to round out this module.

Tone Generator

This will add a sine wave to any incoming signal and offers Envelope, Bend, and Shape control settings.

Figure 4.46

Drum Module Panel

The Drum module panel was reviewed earlier in this chapter, with regard to loading drum patches. Now, let's examine the global parameters this module has to offer.

Figure 4.47

Offset

Pitch and Decay Offset are global controls that affect all modules used in the Drum and FX section. By adjusting pitch or decay, any applicable parameters can be adjusted as well.

For instance, lowering the Decay Offset will cause not only the decay of any drum module, but also can be applied to any FX device containing a Decay parameter.

Send

This section controls the level of sound sent to the Bus FX module. In addition, the Kong also offers Aux 1 and 2, which allow the signal to be routed outside via Kong to other devices in Reason.

Level, Tone, and Pan

These control the overall level, tone, and pan positions of the entire Drum module.

Pad Settings

Pad settings offer control over a variety of useful functions as they pertain to each of the sixteen pads.

Mute/Solo

This controls the status of solo and mute for any given pad. There is also a dedicated Clear button that removes multiple soloed or muted pads simultaneously.

Pad Groups

There are nine pad groups, broken up into three categories; Mute, Link, and Alt.

Mute

Mute groups (A, B, and C) cause any pad assigned to mute any other pad within the same group. For instance, if you assign Pads 1 and 2 to Mute Group A, then hitting either Pad 1 or 2 will cause the previous triggered pad to be muted. This is useful for creating realistic high-hat patterns, where a closed high-hat sound would mute an open high-hat sound.

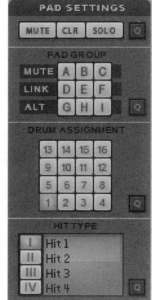

Figure 4.48

Link

Link groups (D, E, and F) cause any assigned pads to trigger simultaneously. For instance, if you assign Pads 3 and 4 to Link Group D, then hitting either Pad 3 or 4 would cause both pads to trigger.

Alt

Alt groups (G, H, and I) will alternate between any pads assigned to a group. For instance, if you assign Pads 9, 10, and 11 to Alt Group G, then hitting any pad in the group would alternate randomly between any of the three assigned pads.

Drum Assignment

The Drum Assignment section allows you to trigger one drum module across multiple pads. This may prove to be quite useful, depending on the type of drum module, as well as the hit type being used.

Hit Type

Depending on which drum module is being used, the Hit Type control affords the ability to trigger different samples or variations of sound.

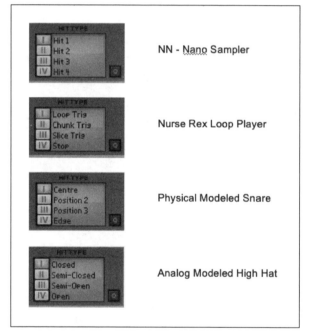

Figure 4.49

Quick Edit

Located across the bottom of each section of the Drum Module control panel and the Pad Settings panel are small boxes labeled Q. When engaged, Quick Edit affords a bird's-eye view of the assignments of specific parameters over all sixteen pads simultaneously.

In figure 4.50, you see the Quick Edit mode of the Pad Drum Assignment.

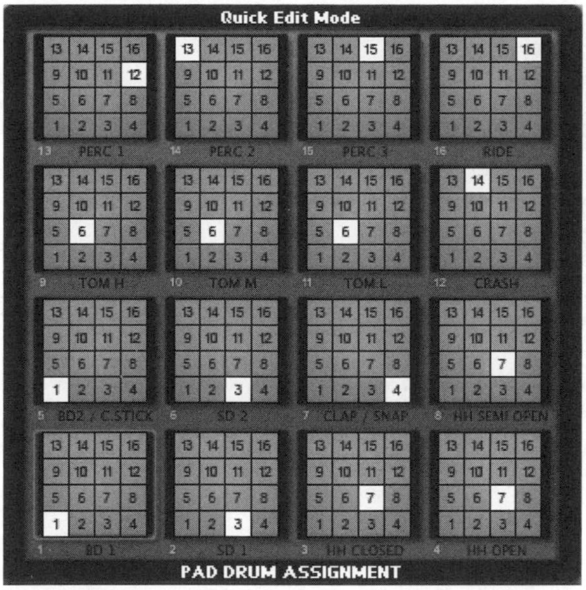

Figure 4.50

Notice that Pad 5 is assigned to Pad 1; and Pads 3, 4, and 8 are assigned to Pad 7.

This means that Pad 1 and 5 share one drum module, while Pads 3, 4, and 8 share another drum module.

Practical Use of Pad Settings

For you to fully grasp the programming potential of pad assignments, let's take a look at the programming of a preset.

- Start by opening the TR404 kit from the Beyer Lekebusch folder located in the Kong Kit folder.
- Once open, click on Pad 1 and open the Show Drum and FX programmer.
- Pad 1 has an NN-Nano Sampler assigned.
- Hit Slot 1 has sample BD_Sturdy loaded into it.
- Hit Slot 2 has sample BD_404Loose loaded into it.
- Next, open the Quick Edit Drum assignment, by hitting the Q button.
- Here you will find Pads 1 and 5 have been assigned to Pad 1.
- Now hit the Quick Edit Hit Type button.
- Here you will find that Pad 1 is assigned to Hit 1, while Pad 5 is assigned to Hit 2.
- The hit type designates which sample is triggered from the NN-Nano Sampler.

Beat Juggling with Nurse Rex

- Begin by selecting Initialize Patch from the Edit menu.
- Next, select Pad 1 and open the Show Drum and FX programmer.
- Select the Nurse Rex Loop Player from the Drum Module drop-down list.
- Then select the BSQ_PhatDrumz_105.rx2 from the Beats folder, found within the Bomb Squad (BSQ) folder, which is located in the Dr. Rex Drum Loops folder.
- Engage the Quick Edit Drum Assignment button and assign Pads 1, 2, 3, 4, and 5 to Pad 1.
- Next, engage the Quick Edit Hit Type button and assign Pads 1 through 4 to Chunk Trigger.

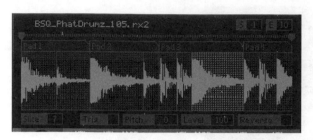

Figure 4.51

Notice how each assignment of the chunk trigger in the Hit Type window is reflected within the display of the Nurse Rex Slice editor.

Playing Pad 5 triggers the entire loop; Pads 1 through 4 trigger sections of the loop. By playing the sections rhythmically, you can approximate a form of beat juggling.

Chapter 5

ADVANCED ROUTING

One of them most fascinating and exhilarating aspects of Reason is the reverse side of the rack. As a teaching tool, it offers a glimpse at how to wire up a physical rack and connect analog synthesizers and sequencers.

Reason offers an unprecedented amount of control in an easy-to-understand format. Other programs offer similar types of control, but you need a degree in computer science to be able to program them. With the basic understanding of control voltage and gate signals and a spirit for experimentation, you will be able to create sounds nothing short of breathtaking.

14:2 Mixer

If you examine the back of the 14:2 mixer, you'll find CV (control voltage) inputs for both Pan and Level control.

Auto-Panning

The Subtractor offers no control for creating an auto-pan effect, as it has only a mono output, but with the use of the Pan CV input on the 14:2 mixer, it's completely possible.

Let's begin by your creating a Subtractor synthesizer and selecting the Omenous patch from the Pads folder.

Tab to the back of your rack and cable LFO 1 from the Modulation output to the Pan CV input for Channel 1.

Use the knob just below the Pan CV input to control the width of the pan. Moving the knob to the left decreases the width, whereas moving it to the right increases the effect.

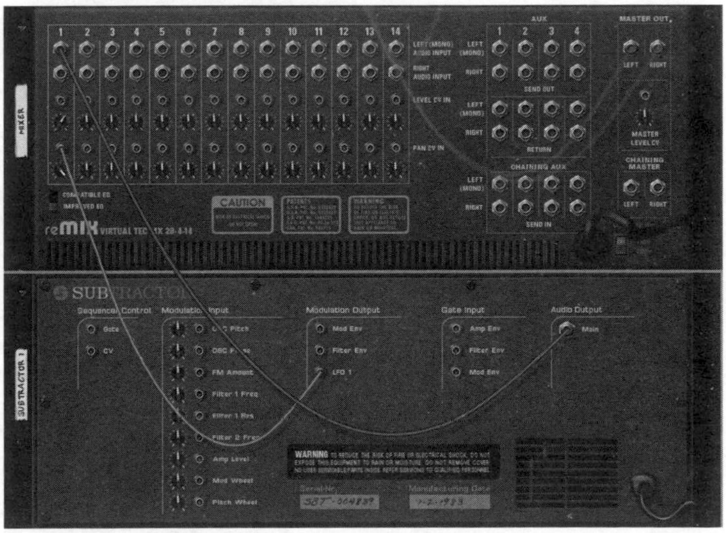

Figure 5.1

You can adjust the waveform and rate of the pan via LFO 1 control parameters, as you normally would. Note that you don't have to increase the amount of the LFO, as the Pan CV knob on the rear of the Mixer controls that.

Auto-Leveling

This offers a tremolo effect achieved by modulation of the level, exactly like modulating the amplifier on the Subtractor. Only LFO 2 has the ability to modulate the Amp circuit, but is somewhat limited with a fixed waveform and no sync.

Use the same instrument and setup you used previously for the auto-pan, only wire LFO 1 from the modulation output to the Level CV input.

Try experimenting with different patches and different waveforms.

A favorite patch for this type of effect is the Outer Mongolia from the Pad folder.

Set LFO 1 to sync at a sixteenth note with a square waveform.

Incidentally, it is possible to create this on the Subtractor itself, by cabling LFO 1 from the modulation output to the Amp Level input of the Modulation Input section.

Complex LFO

This is a useful patch that combines the signals of different LFOs to create a modulation truly unique and unpredictable.

Begin by selecting patch Wheel Wah Lead from the Monosynth Folder for the Subtractor.

If you remember, holding Shift down while creating an instrument, prevents any auto-cabling.

Hold Shift down while creating a Spider CV, Subtractor, and Malstrom.

Next, cable LFO 1 from the Wheel Wah Lead to the first input of the Spider CV merge section.

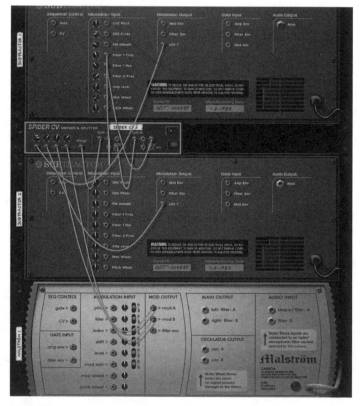

Figure 5.2

Next, do the same for the Subtractor 2 to the second input.

Finally, cable mods A and B from the Malstrom to the third and fourth inputs of the Spider CV.

Cable the merge output to the Split A input of the Spider CV.

Now, cable from Split A output to the Filter 1 Freq input of the Wheel Wah Lead Subtractor.

Also cable the Inv output of Split A to Filter 1 Res.

In Fig. 5.2, I cabled the Inv out to a Split B input and then routed a Split B output to the Filter 1 Res. This gives you multiple outputs of the inverted signal to route to other parameters or additional devices. You could create an additional Spider CV device for additional splits to route to other devices and instruments.

If you like this patch and wish to be able to access the setup quickly, try combining everything into a Combinator.

Simply Shift-click each instrument and device, and select Combine from the Edit menu. Save the Combinator as a custom patch and it's now a sonic tool in your arsenal.

Tunable Feedback

Sometimes you're looking for not-so-pretty sounds, such as the sound of feedback from an electric guitar. This particular patch emulates the scraping of the pick on a guitar string and is followed by feedback, which can be played by your MIDI controller keyboard.

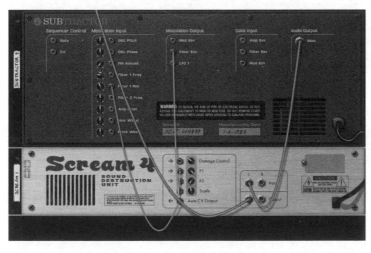

Figure 5.3

Start by creating a Subtractor and selecting the Bass Guitar patch.

Next, create a Scream 4 Sound Destruction Unit. The auto cabling should have cabled the output of the Subtractor into the Scream 4, and from the Scream 4 into an available channel on the mixer.

On the Scream 4, select EasyFuzz from the Instrument Tweaks folder. Next, adjust the Damage Type to Modulate.

On the rear of the rack, cable the Filter Env from the Modulation Output to the P1 input of the Scream. Turn the P1 knob all the way to the right.

Next, route the Auto CV Output of the Scream 4 to the Filter 1 Res of the Subtractor.

Sequenced Stutter Vocal Sample

Any vocal sample will do. I chose a simple two-syllable sample Bad Bwoy to work with.

- Create a NN-XT sampler and initialize from the Edit menu.
- From the Remote editor, click the Browse Sample button and select the vocal sample.
- Next, open the Song Sample tab from the Tool window.
- Select the sample from the Assigned > NN-XT and click Duplicate.
- Next, hit Edit on the original. Once the Edit window is open, click the Snap Sample Start/ End to Transient selection and move the End position of the sample so that it ends before the Bwoy portion. Rename the sample Bad and hit Save.
- On the duplicate sample, move the Start position so that it starts with the Bwoy portion.
- You should now have two samples labeled Bad and Bwoy.

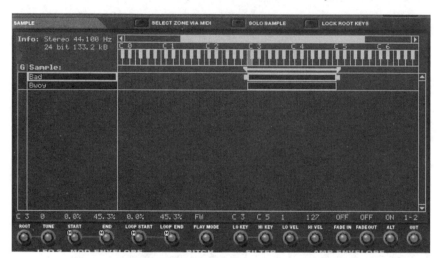

Figure 5.4

- On the NN-XT, click the Bad sample zone and select Duplicate Zone.
- Click the Browse Sample button, navigate to the Song Sample section, and select Bwoy.
- Next, click the sample zone group so that both samples are selected.
- With both samples selected, turn the Alt knob to On. Now, as the keys are pressed, the sample alternates between Bad and Bwoy.
- With the NN-XT selected, create an RPG-8.
- Set the Mode to Random, Octave to 2, and adjust the rate to eighth notes.

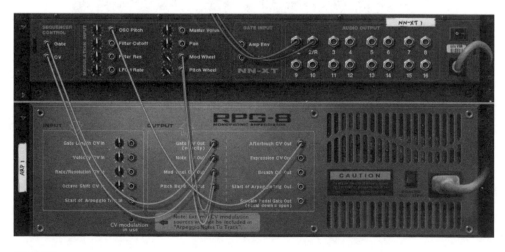

Figure 5.5

- Tab to the rear of the rack.
- Cable the Aftertouch CV Out to the Osc Pitch input.
- Play C3 on your MIDI keyboard controller. You will hear the Bad Boy sample play randomly at different octaves.
- If your keyboard has Aftertouch, pressing harder will cause the pitch to increase. By pressing rhythmically, you can create glitched vocals sounds.
- If you wish to save this patch, you must detach the samples.
- To do this, select Song Self Contain Settings from the File menu and deselect Bad and Bwoy from the sample list.

BV512 Digital Vocoder

Vocoders, or voice encoders, were developed in the 1930s and used widely during WWII to help with communications over long distances and encrypting messages.

The application of music was first attempted in the mid- to late '50s, but didn't reach mainstream consciousness until the late '60s/early '70s, by way of electronic musicians such as Kraftwerk.

The most famous sound of the vocoder is the talking synthesizer, or "robot voice," but many unique sounds are possible.

The technology involves a carrier and modulator signal. The carrier is the base of the sound, while the modulator acts as an envelope follower, controlling several multiband filters. The more bands available, the more intelligible or precise the vocoding will be.

Let's begin by creating a Malstrom synthesizer and a Dr. OctoRex Loop Player.

For this example, you can pick whatever patches you'd like, but I find sounds with lots of harmonic content and rhythm really helps when making an interesting and effective patch.

I chose the Screech MW from the Monosynths folder for the Malstrom and the KLB Percussion/BongoBoom patch found under the Dr. OctoRex Patches > Percussion > Keith LeBlanc folder.

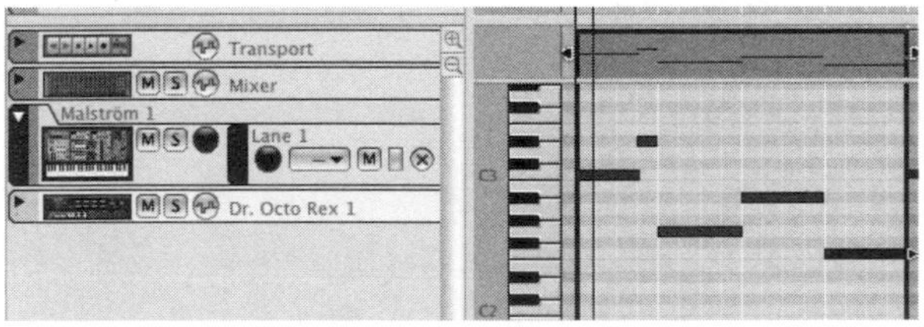

Figure 5.6

In Fig. 5.6, I recorded a simple sequence with the notes C3, D#3, G2, A#2, and F2. Feel free to use any sequence that works for your production.

Next, with the Malstrom synthesizer selected, create a BV512 Digital Vocoder. The Malstrom will auto-cable itself to the carrier input of the BV512, while the BV512 will cable itself to the mixer input.

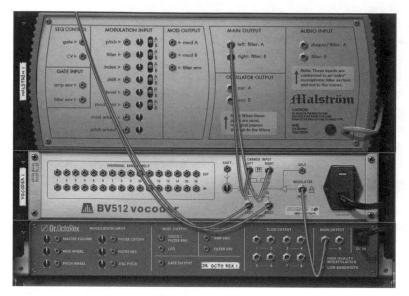

Figure 5.7

Tab to the back of the rack and route the left side of the Main Out of the Dr. OctoRex to the Modulation Input of the BV512.

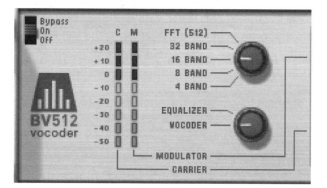

Figure 5.8

Tab to the front of the rack to explore some parameters on the BV512.

The two LED meters represent the carrier signal (C) and the modulation signal (M).

The knob on the upper left allows for band selection, with a range of 4, 8, 16, 32, and 512 (FFT).

The 512 (FFT) uses a different method of analysis called Fast Fourier Transform, which works at a much higher resolution and offers the best intelligibility when synthesizing vocals. It does tend to be slower than the other band settings and is not as ideal for processing drums and rhythmic content.

The knob below the band selection changes from Vocoder mode to an Equalizer mode. This is not a high-fidelity EQ, but one that offers some harsh tonal adjustments.

The center section offers a visual graph of the modulations levels on the top portion, while the frequency band levels may be adjusted along the bottom. The number of bands selected will be reflected in the number of frequency band levels you can adjust. The 512 (FFT) selection gives you thirty-two bands, each band representing sixteen bands per level adjustment in a linear fashion. The lower frequencies are on the left side of the interface, increasing to higher frequencies as you move to the right.

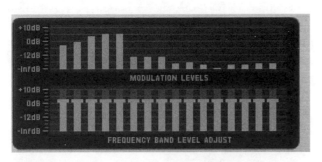

Figure 5.9

Adjusting the level bands can increase the amplitude of the entire sound or just the chosen frequencies.

Figure 5.10

The top portion, which includes Hold, Attack, and Decay, affects the envelope follower parameters. Increasing the Attack softens the overall sound, whereas increasing the Release brings a more legato feel.

The Hold button freezes the envelope at a specific time. CV control is available from the rear of the unit. Using an LFO or Matrix sequencer can create really interesting rhythmic effects beyond just the parameters available on the BV512.

The Shift parameter shifts the carrier signal up and down and can create phaser-style effects.

The HF Emphasis knob boosts the high frequencies in the carrier signal, giving the tone of the overall sound a more cutting edge.

The Dry/Wet controls the balance between the modulator and vocoded sound. This should be left fully wet for classic vocoder applications.

In addition to sequencing with the BV512, it is possible to vocode in real time with the use of a microphone.

This involves routing from the physical input to the modulator input on the synth, and connecting a microphone to the appropriate input.

This allows you to create the singing synthesizer sounds often heard in bands such as Trans Am.

The Side Chain Bass Line

The use of side chaining is often used in various style of music. Let's take a look at a side chain bass line often heard in progressive and tech house tracks. It often sounds as if the bass sounds are in reverse and has a "sucking" quality to it.

The concept is simple. The bass synthesizer is run through a compressor, only the compressor is being triggered by another source via its side chain input.

Create a Malstrom synthesizer and load the Killer Bass patch from the Bass folder.

With the Malstrom selected, create an MClass compressor.

The MClass compressor will automatically cable itself between the Malstrom's outputs and the mixers inputs.

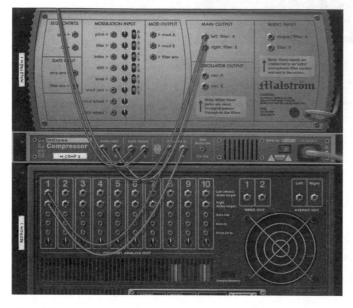

Figure 5.11

Next, create a ReDrum. Cable the stereo output of the ReDrum to the Side Chain input of the compressor.

On the MClass compressor, set Ratio to its highest setting (infinite:1).

Lower the Threshold to the left.

The Attack should be at its fastest setting, fully left, while the Release should be set fully right.

Figure 5.12

On the ReDrum, program a quarter-note kick drum pattern, using buttons 1, 5, 9, and 13.

Finally, record a bass line for the Malstrom track. You'll hear the classic side chain bass line.

Analog Drum Sequencer

This is an available template document that ships with Reason that uses the ReDrum's sequencer to trigger ten Subtractors.

Figure 5.13

To open, select Open from the File menu and navigate to the Template folder, found in the Reason folder.

Then, click the Run button on the ReDrum transport. You'll hear a very basic pattern playing.

Tab to the rear of the rack to examine the wiring.

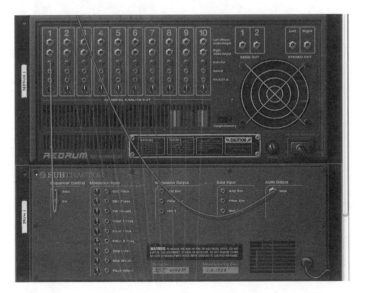

Figure 5.14

In Fig. 5.14, you find the Gate output of Channel 1 on the ReDrum is routed to the Gate input of the Subtractor's sequencer control. The audio output of the Subtractor 1 is routed to the mixer.

This method of sequencing can be used with any of the instruments within Reason.

Chapter 6
ADVANCED SEQUENCING

Advanced Sequencing

In this chapter, you will explore some advanced sequencing techniques that will speed up your workflow and achieve ever more professional results.

The basics of sequencing were already covered in the first Quick Pro Guide book of this series, whose focus was recording, editing, and building up an arrangement.

You'll begin by looking at a new way of building an arrangement utilizing blocks. But first, you will examine the instruments used to create your song.

I used several custom instruments that were created in the synthesis and instrument chapters. You'll recognize the Vocode Bass and the Analog Drum Sequencer that was used previously in the advanced routing chapter.

I have also incorporated several variations of the Wobble Bass that was created in the Malstrom section of the instrument chapter.

Along the way, you will be adding some other instruments to fill out your production.

To participate effectively in the following process, you will first need to download and open the song "Under the Gun," found on the Hal Leonard website under Quick Pro Guides: Sound Design and Advanced Sequencing.

Figure 6.1

In Fig. 6.1, you will find a shot of my work environment. Notice how I've detached the sequencer from the rack. This provides more room to sequence and edit, while keeping my rack within my visual range. The use of a larger or second monitor can provide greater enhancement of your working capabilities.

To detach or reattach the sequencer, simply select the second button in the upper right corner of the sequencer window.

Figure 6.2

The Sequence Window

In the sequencer window, you will see ten tracks, most with MIDI clips. If you were to try and edit any of these tracks, you find that the MIDI clips are not accessible from the Song view. It's because the clips were assembled in Block view, a new arrangement feature found in Reason.

Block View

Working with Blocks is very similar to working with patterns on a drum machine. Any number of tracks with recorded sequenced materials can be easily and quickly replicated throughout your song. Any new MIDI clips recorded from the Song mode will override the data contained in a block. This allows variations on the data to be created easily throughout the entire song.

You first must make sure that the Blocks option is enabled on the transport window. When Blocks is enabled, you can view a single block by entering Block View.

On the upper left corner of the sequencer window, you can see the Song, Block, and Edit buttons. These controls allow you to switch among the different modes.

Figure 6.3

To do so, click the Block button or use the key command B.

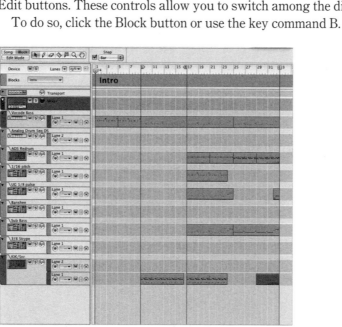

Figure 6.4

In Fig. 6.4, you'll find the Block view of Block 1, titled Intro. The Intro block is thirty-two bars long. You will notice there are the Left and Right locators and an End marker. Without the loop button engaged on the transport window, the sequence will automatically loop between the Start and End markers. The L and R locators allow for looping a section within the block, for the purpose of editing and arranging.

Intro

Figure 6.5

To rename a block, double-click on the title in the colored bar running across the top of the Block View window and input the name you wish to designate.

On the track list in the upper left corner is a box labeled Intro. Clicking in this box reveals a drop-down list of thirty-two available blocks. From here, select Main 1 (Staccato).

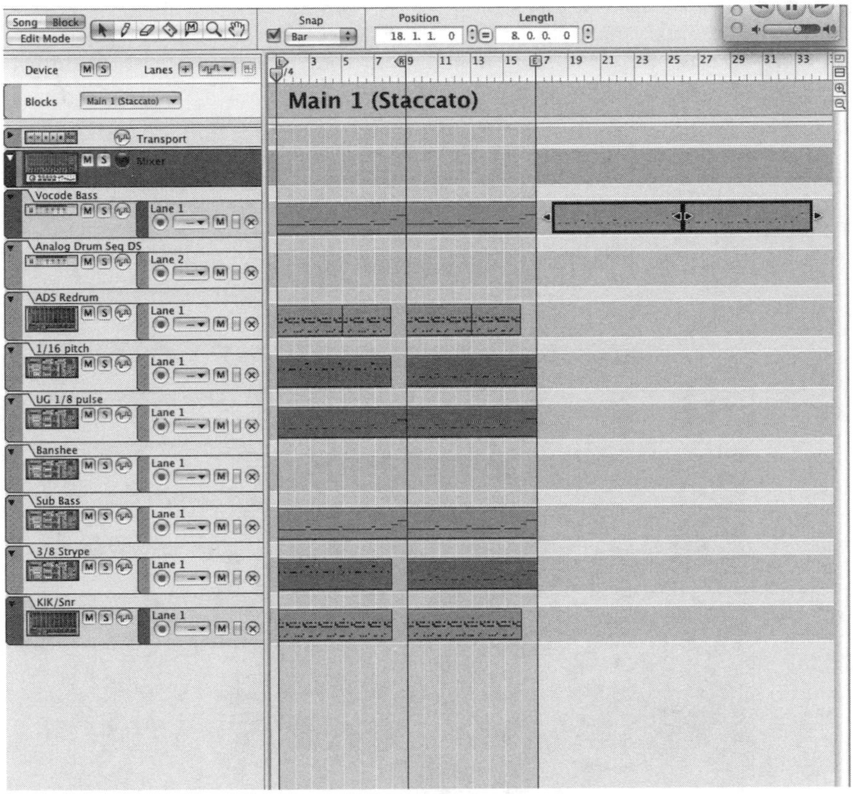

Figure 6.6

In the Main 1 (Staccato) block, you will find a sixteen-bar sequence. Notice the two MIDI clips outside the range of the block. They were set aside when sequencing. These clips have no bearing on the block payback from the Song view.

Recording and editing function the same in Blocks as they do when working in Song mode. To edit a MIDI clip, simply double-click to open Editor View.

A quick method for toggling between Edit mode and Block view is to use the quick key command Shift + Tab. The MIDI editors are only available within the mode from which they originated. For example, you can only edit MIDI data created in Blocks mode from the Block view. The same can be said for any data recorded in Song view.

Block Sequencing

From Song mode, you can see the blocks arranged in the Blocks track at the top of the arrangement window.

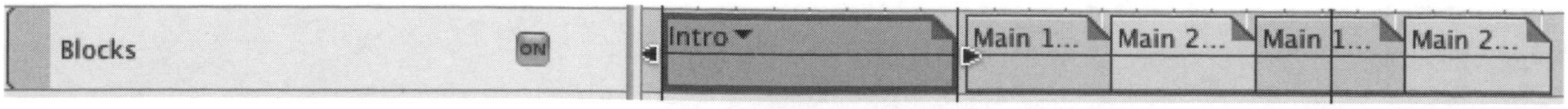

Figure 6.7

To create a new block, click with the Pencil tool. The first block is always the default clip. Click on the name of the block to reveal the drop-down list, to select a different clip. It is also possible to use the Click and Drag option to copy a block into a new destination. When copying, be sure to click on the bottom half of the block, below the block name.

The Rack

Before you finish building out the arrangement of your song, take a moment to confirm the instruments used in the creation of your song so far. An easy way to listen to each instrument is to set up a loop around the Main 2 (Legato) section and solo each track on the mixer.

Vocode Bass

The Vocode Bass is based on the patch you made in chapter 5, utilizing the BV512 Digital Vocoder.

Figure 6.8

In this updated patch, which combined into a Combinator, you have a Malstrom and Dr. OctoRex Loop Player cabled through two Spider audio splitters and routed through two BV512 Digital Vocoders. The top vocoder is set to thirty-two bands, while the bottom is set to four bands. Both BV512s are routed into a micro mix, combining their signals into a single stereo output.

Analog Drum Sequencer DS

This is a monster of a patch that has been modified from the standard template found in the Reason folder. The patch consists of a ReDrum using its Gate Out function to trigger drum sounds from a Kong and several Subtractors.

Figure 6.9

In Fig. 6.9, you'll see the heart of the Analog Drum Sequencer, the ReDrum. The ReDrum has a four-bar sequence programmed to trigger a Kick, Snare, Lowtom, Claydrum, High Hat, and Ride Cymbal.

If you look at the mixer, you will find that Kick and Snare have been rerouted to the main mixer, bypassing the submixer. This allows for more control over the kick and snare sound, and offers the other drums the benefit of submixing with compression and limiting.

In creating this, I used the Copy Pattern to Track function from the Edit menu, to allow for easier sequencing and editing from the arrangement window.

Figure 6.10

In Fig. 6.10, you'll see the Bass Drum has been altered by increasing the Decay and Release parameters of the Amp Env to shape the sound to more of an 808 kick drum. The output of the Bass Drum is routed through the MClass Compressor, while the side chain input is being used to create a subtle rhythmic effect.

The Snare sound is afforded by the Kong Drum designer. It features two Snare samples assigned to Pads 3 and 4 and linked to trigger as one. These samples were taken from the ReDrum > xclusive drums-sorted folder.

Figure 6.11

In Fig. 6.11, you'll see the Analog Drum Sequencer interface with the programmer. Note the Drum 1 assignment of Amp Env Decay and Amp Env Release to Rotary 1 in the programmer. This setting allows for quick control in which to shape the sound of the kick drum.

Kik/Snr ReDrum

The primary kick drum sound comes from this ReDrum with House Kit 7 loaded on to it.

Figure 6.12

The ReDrum is triggered from the MIDI clip generated by the Analog Drum Sequencer in the arrangement window. The MIDI clip was copied on to the Kik/Snr track. Note the muted tracks featured on the ReDrum.

I've also routed the S1 and S2 from the Kick Drum sound on Channel 1 to a Spider Audio device, to trigger the side chain input of compressors connected to the Kick Drum from the Analog Drum Sequencer and the Sub Bass.

Sub Bass

The Malstrom set with a simple sine wave output provides the sub bass for your track. In fact, this same patch was originally created at the end of the Malstrom section in chapter 2 of this book.

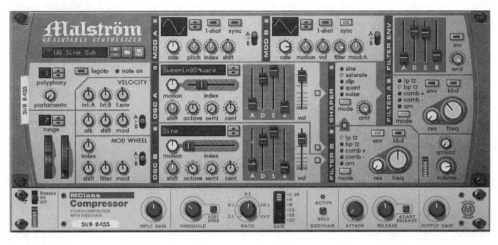

Figure 6.13

During this procedure, you created a patch with a SweepingSquare waveform and a sine wave. If you recall, you routed Osc B to a separate channel on the mixer. As you can infer from this case, it's much easier to create a new patch dedicated to the sub bass on the mixer. The output of the Sub Bass patch is routed through an MClass compressor, with the side chain input triggered by the kick from the Kik/Snr ReDrum patch. The side chain allows the kick drum to push the sub bass down in volume for an instant, giving the kick drum more presence without modifying the EQ.

UG Pulse 1/8

The UG Pulse 1/8 patch is the original Wobble Bass patch created in chapter 2, minus any Osc B sine wave output. It provides a rhythmic anchor in your song.

Figure 6.14

The Main 1 block triggers the UG Pulse 1/8 with staccato notes. In block Main 2, with the longer legato notes, it generates a driving eighth-note pattern that's caused by modulating Filter A by Mod B.

Banshee

The Banshee patch is another variation from your original Wobble Bass.

Figure 6.15

The Osc A sample is changed to PlasticPipe, the octave parameter is raised to 6, and the subtle shift setting is –4.

Filter A is modulated at a 1sixteenth-note rate.

Figure 6.16

On the main mixer, note that the Banshee channel is set to hard-pan left. Aux 1 is sending the signal to a DDL-1, thereby creating an excellent panning effect with the panning setting at hard right.

UG Pitch 1/16

The UG Pitch 1/16 is a variation on the Wobble Bass patch in which Mod B modulates the Filter at a sixteenth-note rate. The pitch is modulated by a stair step waveform in Mod A, at a quarter-note rate.

UG Strype 3/8

The UG Strype 3/8, also based on the Wobble Bass patch, offers a unique effect by modulating Filter A at a rate of three-eighth notes. Additional modulation by Mod A of the Shift parameter at 8/4 affords a unique sound and rhythm effect to any arrangement.

Figure 6.17

Building the Arrangement

Now you will resume building out this arrangement by creating a breakdown and outro, and by adding a few other elements to round out the track.

The Breakdown

For the breakdown, you will create a sequence somewhat based on the intro.

- The first step is to copy from the intro until Bar 98, or just after the Main 2 block.
- Click on Block or press B to enter Block mode.
- With the Intro block in view, select all the MIDI clips present and use the key command Control + C (PC) or Command + C (Mac) to copy the content to your clipboard.
- Next, select Block 4 from the drop-down menu.
- Rename Block 4 Breakdown by double-clicking the name displayed in the bar at the top of the window.
- With the SPL set at Bar 1, use the Paste key command, Control + V (PC) or Command + V (Mac), to complete this step. Next, you will make some modifications with a series of deletes as follows:

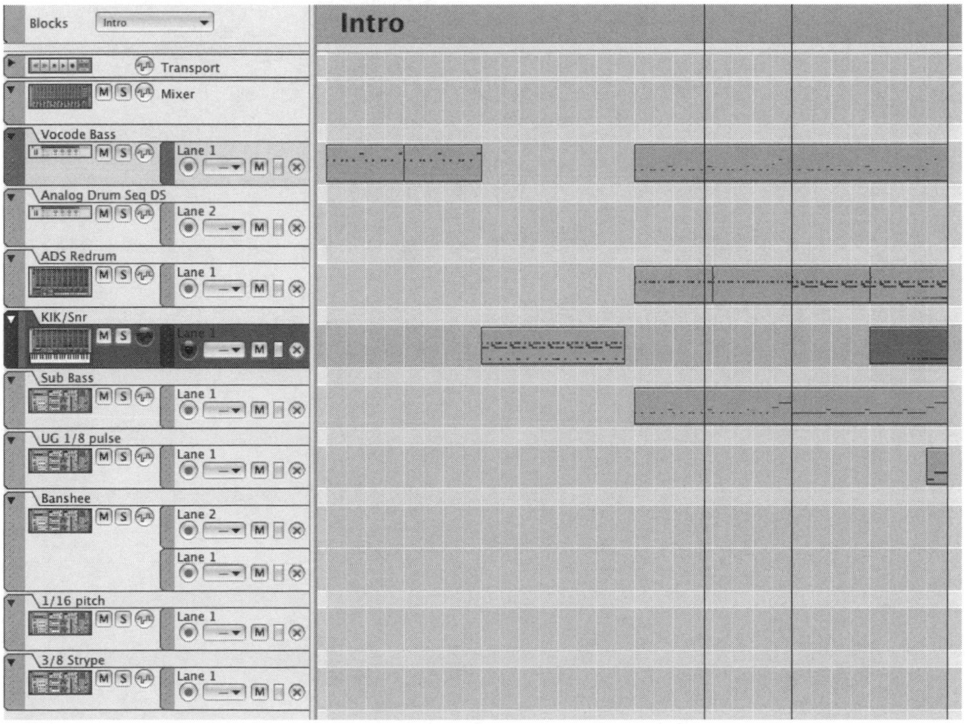

Figure 6.18

- Delete the Vocode Bass Clip, starting at Bar 9.
- Delete the Kick/Snr Clip, starting at Bar 17.
- Delete the UG Pulse 1/8, starting at Bar 17.
- Delete the 1/16 Pitch, starting at Bar 17.

Next, you will continue using a series of steps designed to further modify the piece.

- First, select all the clips from Bar 17 to Bar 33 and move them to Bar 9.
- Then, move the End marker (E) to Bar 25.
- Copy the Sub Bass MIDI clip at Bar 17 to the Banshee track at Bar 9.
- Now, you will need to select the Banshee clip at Bar 9 and transpose it down –24 semitones. This can be executed manually from the Key editor or by using the Sequencer Tools tab from the Tool window.

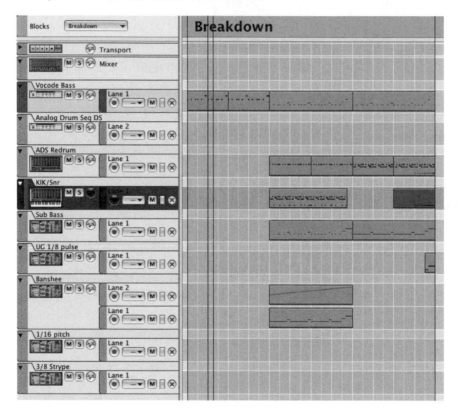

Figure 6.19

- Next, create a new lane for the Banshee track by clicking the + Lane button at the top of the track column.
- At Bar 9, record some pitch bend data.
- Now, adjust the newly recorded clip to be eight bars and double-click to enter the Edit window.

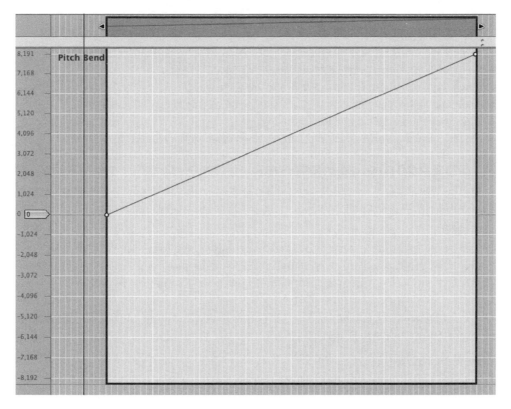

Figure 6.20

- Next, either draw or edit the pitch bend data to re-create the image shown in Fig. 6.20.

The Outro

The outro is another variation of the intro, only instead of building up the sounds over time, the sounds will drop out.

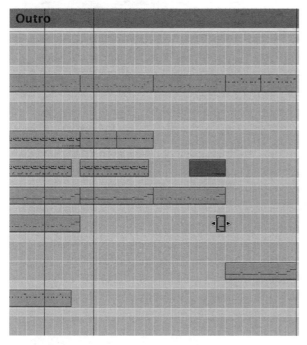

Figure 6.21

- First, swap the first two Vocode Bass MIDI clips with the last clip that starts at Bar 25.
- Now, on the ADS ReDrum track, move the two MIDI clips beginning at Bar 17 to Bar 1, and position the last ADS ReDrum clip (Kick Drum Roll) to end at Bar 25.
- For the Kik/Snr track, move the second clip at Bar 17 to Bar 1.
- Move the last Sub Bass Clip to Bar 1 and copy it to Bar 9.
- Then, move the UG 1/8 pulse to Bar 1 and the small Clip at Bar 32 to Bar 24.
- Now, move the 1/16 pitch to Bar 1.
- Finally, copy the Sub Bass Clip at Bar 1 to the Banshee track at Bar 25.

Adding Additional Elements.

Now that you have finalized the basic structure, let's add a few more elements to give your track a little more ear candy.

Sound FX

Notice the gap that is present at Bar 33 just before the Main block begins. You are going to record a sound effect to fill in this gap and create effect.

First, create a Combinator and load Hyperspace Explosion from the Synth FX folder.

Record a two-bar sequence at Bar 33. You will need to move all the blocks over one measure, from Bar 34 to Bar 35.

Reverse Crash

Listeners to your track will appreciate a reverse effect to signal an impending transition in the track. A great way to achieve this effect is to use a reverse crash cymbal.

Create an NN-XT and initialize the patch. Then, load a crash cymbal from the ReDrum > xclusive drums-sorted > 06 Cymbals folder.

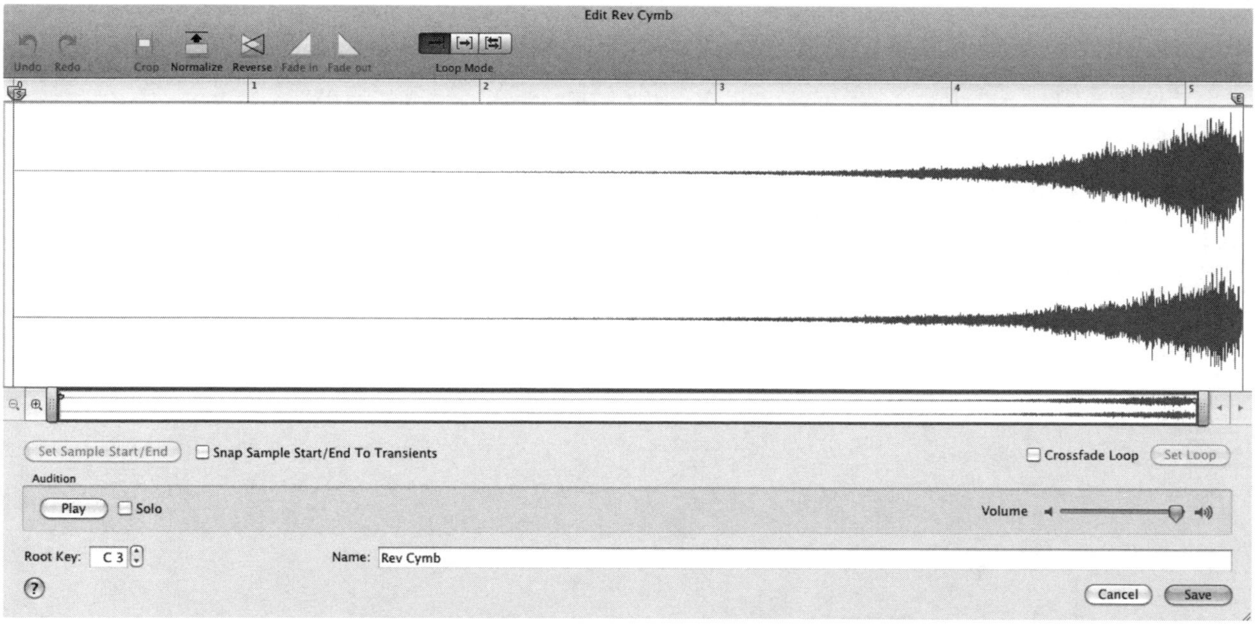

Figure 6.22

Once this is loaded, navigate your way to the Sample Tool tab of the Tool window.

Now, select the NN-XT > Crash Cymbal and press the Edit button.

Next, press the Reverse button and save the sample using the title Rev Crash.

Now you need to record a MIDI clip of the newly created Rev Crash. It's important to make sure that the end of clip you create lines up to align with the end of the sample.

Align the end of the clip with Bars 33, 99, 123, 187, and 211.

Dr. Rex Tabla

Adding a Tabla loop to the second half of your track will give a subtle edge that creates an innate ambiance of variation.

First, create a Dr. OctoRex and load it with Percussion/Tabla 75–3 from the Percussion folder.

Press the Run button and listen to the first loop entitled Tabla_08_Introl_075.

Notice that although the loop has the right rhythm, it is out of tune with the rest of your track.

Figure 6.23

Now, adjust Global Transpose to –5 on the bottom right side of the Dr. OctoRex panel.

Set the L and R locators to frame the Main 1 block.

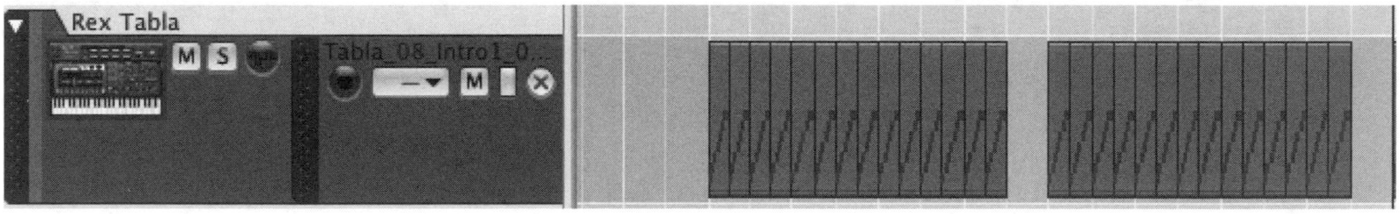

Figure 6.24

Unfold the Dr. OctoRex programmer and click the Copy Pattern to Track button.

Next, remove or delete two clips at the end of every eight bars.

Then, copy the sequence of clips to the rest of the Main 1 and 2 block sections, from Bar 123 to Bar 187.

Noisy Bugz

Last, let's add one final effect element to your track.

First, create a Combinator and load Noisy Bugz from the Synth FX folder.

Figure 6.25

On the main panel of the Combinator, deselect the Noise button by pressing it.

Figure 6.26

Next, record a clip for the Main 1 block. Each note should be at G3 for a duration set to 0.2.1.0.

Next, enter Block mode for the Main 2 (Legato) and copy the first clip from the Banshee track. Paste the clip onto the Noisy Bugz track, located under the Main 2 section.

Figure 6.27

Finally, copy the MIDI clips to the other Main 1 and 2 sections in the second half of the song. Play it back—and enjoy the enhancements created in the last section and imagine all that you can do with your production using these techniques.

In the next chapter, we will examine more closely some advanced mixing techniques.

Chapter 7
ADVANCED MIXING TECHNIQUES

Truth be told, this is my absolute favorite part of the song creation process. If you compare arrangement and sequencing to be like sketching out an idea for a painting, then mixing is equivalent to breaking out the brushes and enhancing that outline into a clear and focused work of art.

When working on a mix, I always find it's best to start well rested and with a fresh set of ears, to ensure an optimal process.

Provided you have been following along through the procedures undertaken during the last chapter, your arrangement and premix should be prepared and ready to go.

If, however, you haven't or are not entirely sure of the resulting arrangement or premix, then simply go to the Hal Leonard website or enclosed DVD and open the "Under the Gun—Chapter 7—Advanced Mixing" to find the properly created song file available for download.

Reference Mix

I also highly recommend utilizing a reference mix during any mixing session. This is a professionally produced and mastered track that you can listen to as needed, to guide how your track should sound.

It's also important to try not to reproduce someone else's track. You are listening to the reference track chiefly to be able to find the right balance of sounds within your own track.

For instance, before I begin working on my own mix, I find it easier for my brain to first identify the sound of correct balance between the kick drum and bass by listening to a properly mixed track. However, if I were to dive into my mixing work without hearing such a reference, it will take a lot more energy and time to achieve the correct balance in my sound.

That being said, to do this I usually look for a reference mix that is similar in style to the track I will be mixing. Genre is most important; for example, it doesn't make sense to use a rock song as a reference for an electronic track.

Once you've selected which reference track to use, make sure to keep it on hand so you can consult it throughout the mixing process. A good practice to adopt is to listen to the reference track for a couple of minutes after every break you take, before you resume work. This will allow you to retune your ears and brain. Remember that it is very important to take regular breaks after every forty-five minutes to an hour while working, to prevent fatigue and ensure you are working in an optimal state.

A reference mix is also useful for setting the appropriate balance of your studio monitors and subwoofer.

Ideally, the listening levels should be set to around 85 dB.

The Big Meter

Before you get into the actual mixing, you will need to set up the Big Meter, found on the Hardware Interface.

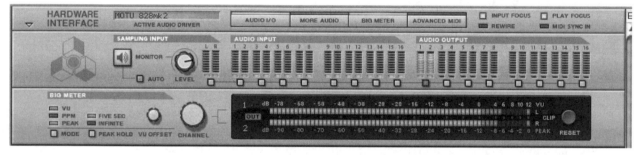

Figure 7.1

Begin by selecting the button located under Audio Output 1 and 2. This button will glow red to indicate when it is selected. This sets the channel that will be displayed by the Big Meter.

Located on the left side of the Big Meter are a number of different parameters, including the Meter modes, Peak Hold settings, VU Offset, and Channel Selection.

VU Meter

The VU meter, or Volume Unit meter, is visual meter based on the design of an average loudness setting. This meter represents the slowest of the three settings, averaging around 300 milliseconds. It's the closest meter to how humans perceive loudness as sound. The original VU meters were designed with a needle and offered a typical range of –20 dB to +3 dB.

PPM Meter

The PPM meter, or Peak Performance meter, is a quasi-peak meter that's faster than the VU meter at 10 milliseconds, but not as fast as the Peak meter. Whereas the VU meter displays an average level between the highest peak and lowest trough, the PPM meter shows a more accurate reading of the peak values. The 10-millisecond response time allows for a different detail of the displayed value, but note that it is still not as accurate as the true Peak meter.

Peak Meter

The Peak meter accurately depicts peak levels with a 0-millisecond response time. Its ultrafast response time instantly displays the highest peaks within the audio signal.

Using the Mode button allows you to cycle through the different types of meters. If you continue to cycle through, it will split the meter, permitting two modes to be displayed at once. The different combinations include VU and Peak, as well as PPM and Peak.

Depending on what element you are working on within the mix, you will be switching among the different settings.

Peak Hold

This offers two settings known as Five Seconds and Infinite.

Five Seconds

This setting will hold the highest Peak setting for five seconds before resetting itself to catch the next highest peak. This is a useful setting for monitoring the peak levels throughout the entire duration of the track.

Infinite

This setting holds the highest registered peak indefinitely. This setting is useful if you are looking for clipping that might have occurred either during a recording session or during the mix-down. Use the Reset button to clear the peaks or clipping from the mix.

VU Offset

The VU Offset knob enables the scaling of the VU meter to permit settings from 0 to +20. You will be maintaining your settings at the default +12 setting during this mixing session.

Channel Selector

The Channel selector allows you to select the channel for the Big Meter. This has already been set by the Selection button, and does not need to be changed.

Clip Indicator

This indicator shows when the output has been, which may occur during the digital clipping process. Use the Reset button to clear the Clip Indicator.

Figure 7.2

Reason uses a floating-point processor for the computation of audio signals, which results in an almost infinite headroom and the inability to clip internally. The clip LEDs indicate when you are in danger of clipping the physical audio hardware, and should be observed.

The Static Mix

During the arrangement section, all of your levels were pretty rough. Because the Default Mastering Suite was engaged during your production, a considerable amount of limiting has occurred.

When you begin your static mix, you'll need to bypass the Mastering Combinator and reset your levels.

A common problem I find when teaching mixing to students is that the levels they try to use are often too high at the start, thereby leaving very little headroom in which to mix properly.

When playing a single track with an output of 0 db, setting the mixer level to 0 db is appropriate.

In this mix session, you will be working with a total of sixteen tracks. If all the levels were set at 0 db, then the output would be too loud and you would incur the risk of the dreaded digital clipping, which often results in an overly harsh distortion.

Although using a compressor or limiter may prevent digital clipping, in such a tradeoff you would be compromising the sound quality, so it is not recommended.

I find it best to adjust all the levels to a combined output of –6 dB. You'll be utilizing the Mastering Suite to polish the mix and ensure your track is loud enough to compete with commercially released tracks. However, it's important to get your static mix in place with an adequate buffer of headroom, to enable the inclusion of additional effects, such as reverb and compression.

Your goal is to achieve an overall balance within the track so that every instrument can be heard appropriately and adequately.

Setting the Mixer

The level faders on the 14:2 mixer have a range of 127. The default setting is 100, but if all levels are left at the default, this setting will result in clipping.

To prevent this, bring all the level meters down to 60. It doesn't have to be an exact setting, so you need not spend an inordinate amount of time on this. Simply lower all level meters to an approximate setting of 60.

Next, bypass the Mastering Combinator. Select a Main 2 section in the latter half of the song, and press P. This sets the L and R locators around the section and begins playing the track in Loop mode.

Already, you should notice that the Banshee track is much louder than the rest of the tracks, so let's lower this setting to 42.

Wrangling the Low End

This track clearly falls within the genre of bass culture. The low end is intended to be somewhat heavy, so you need to ensure the kicks and sub sittings are just right before introducing any additional instruments.

Figure 7.3

The basic EQ on the 14:2 mixer is adequate for removing frequencies, but I do not recommend it for adding treble or bass to any track.

- Start by soloing the Kik/Snr and the Sub Bass tracks.
- Set the Kik/Snr level to 65 and the Sub Bass level to 73.
- Next, remove a bit of the low frequency from these tracks, using the EQ on the mixer.
- Set the bass for the Kik/Snr track to –22 and the Sub Bass track to –22. Don't forget to engage the EQ by selecting the On button.
- Add the ADS Kick track by selecting the Solo setting.
- Now, release the Solo setting on the Sub Bass track, and then set the solo setting to the ADS Kick track on Channel 9. Set this level to 67.
- The ADS Kick appears to be a little too long, so adjust the BD Decay knob to 30 on the Analog Drum Sequencer Combinator.
- Now, remove a little of the bass by enabling the EQ on the ADS Kick track and setting the Bass knob to –10.
- Now, set the Sub Bass to Solo again. You should now hear the Kik/Snr, Sub Bass, and ADS Kick all playing together.
- Note that the Sub Bass and ADS Kick are being processed through MClass compressors. The Kik (from the Kik/Snr), via the side chain input, is triggering each compressor. This produces a dynamic rhythmic effect, which adds a bouncy element to the track.
- These elements make up the majority of the bass frequencies for your song. The rest of the tracks will have most the bass frequencies cut, by comparison.

Add Drums and Percussion

- You will now add the Kong Snare track to your soloed group.
- Adjust the level to 71 and the bass EQ to –20.
- Then, add the Analog Drum Sequencer on channel 2 to the solo group and adjust the level to 76 with the bass EQ set to –46.
- Finally, add the Rex Tabla track on Channel 13 to the solo group and adjust the level to 62 and the bass EQ to –40.

Add the Synthesizers

First, release the Solo setting on all the tracks and start from the beginning.

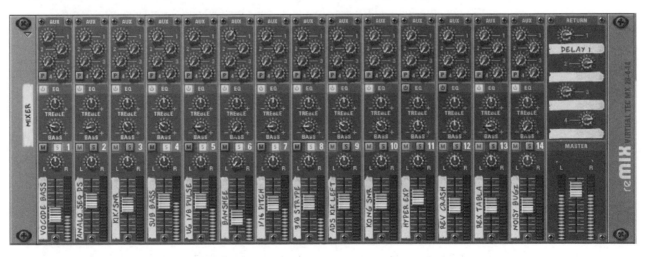

Figure 7.4

- Loop the intro section of the song and set the Vocode Bass to solo on Channel 1.
- Looking at the Big Meter with the PPM and Peak view, you can see that the balance is off between the left and the right.

- Unfold the Vocode Bass Combinator and select the Show Devices button. Set the panning for Vocoder 1 to –20 and for Vocoder 2 to 21.
- Next, set the level for Vocoder 1 to 100 and for Vocoder 2 to 105.
- Decrease the setting of the Master knob to 66.
- On the 14:2 mixer, set the Vocode Bass level to 42 and the bass EQ to –32.
- Now, set a loop around a Main 2 block and add the UG 1/8 Pulse to the solo group.
- Raise the level of the UG 1/8 Pulse track to 74 and set the bass EQ to –40.
- Next, add the Sub Bass and the 1/16 Pitch on Channel 7 to the solo group.
- Set the level for 1/16 Pitch to 68 and the bass EQ to –40.
- Now, add the Banshee track to the solo group, and adjust the level to 34 and the bass EQ to –64.

Finally, add the 3/8 Strype track to the solo group, and set the level to 69 and the bass EQ to –40.

It's important when adding sounds and EQ to do so while considering the context of the track.

Add FX

To begin the next part of the mixing process, you will once again turn off the Loop function and release the Solo setting on all the tracks.

- Start from the beginning of the song.
- First, adjust the level for the Hyper Explosion track on Channels 11 to 82. The Hyper Explosion is the only tracking playing between Bar 33 and bar 35. The level is already higher, so there is no need to remove any bass frequencies.
- At Bar 122, introduce the Noisy Bugz track. Raise the level to 76 and set the bass EQ to –64.
- Now, set a loop around the Rev Crash MIDI clip and set Channel 12 to solo.
- Select the 14:2 mixer and create a RV7000 reverb.
- The RV7000 will automatically cable itself to Aux 2.
- Next, set the Rev Crash level to 62 and the bass EQ to –26.
- On the RV7000, select patch EFX Scary Verb and adjust the Decay to 63, the HF Damp to 23, and the HI EQ to 23.
- Enable the Remote Programmer and adjust the Left and Right Delays to 10 ms.
- Now, give the RV7000 a new name, Rev Crash Veb.
- Then, select the 14:2 and create another RV7000.
- On this RV7000, select patch EKO Space Echo 1.
- Set the Decay to 100.
- Next, enable the Remote Programmer and adjust the Echo time to 4/16.
- Give this RV7000 a new name, Space Echo.
- Increase Aux 3 on Channel 8 and the 3/8 Strype track to 38.
- Also, increase Aux 3 on Channel 11 and Hyper Explosion to 65.
- Last, select the 14:2 mixer and create one more RV7000.
- On this RV7000, select the patch called All Apollo.
- Set the Decay to 100 and rename it Apollo.
- Set Aux 4 on Channel 7, 1/16 Pitch, to 85.
- Then, set Aux 4 on Channel 6, Banshee, to 95.
- Finally, set the Aux 4 on Channel 11, Hyper Explosion, to 99.

The Dynamic Mix

Now that you've got a solid static mix to work with, let's try adding some automation, to animate the song.

Adding Automation to Blocks

The great thing about adding automation to blocks is that this process only needs to be done once. Anytime a block is copied, the automation is also copied as well. Plus, if you decide later that you would prefer to modify any part, you can easily override the automation from the Song Arrangement window.

Figure 7.5

- Begin by entering Block mode and selecting Main 1 (Staccato).
- Right-click, or Control-click, the level fader on Channel 4 of the 14:2 mixer.
- From the drop-down menu, select Edit Automation.
- A new lane will appear on the mixer track.
- With the Pencil tool, draw in a one-bar clip at Bar 8.
- Then, still using the Pencil tool, draw a single node by clicking on Bar 8.
- Next, using the Selector tool, adjust the level to 76.
- Click on the background to back out of the Edit mode for the selected clip.
- Next, right-click, or Control-click, on the level fader located on Channel 5.
- Now Option + Drag the automation clip to copy it from Channel 4 level lane to Channel 5 level lane.
- Double-click the automation clip on Channel 5 and adjust the level node to 87.
- Finally, select both automation clips and Option + Drag to create a copy at Bar 16.
- Now, repeat the same process for Main 2 (Legato).
- Before leaving Main 1, select an automation clip on Channel 5 level and copy to the clipboard by pressing Control + C.
- Now, select Main 2 from the block drop-down list.

- Next, place the SPL at Bar 8 and paste from the clipboard using Control + V.
- Then double-click on the automation clip and adjust the level node to 78.

Adding Automation to Song View

Now you are going to add some automation to the Vocode Bass track in the Intro, Outro, and Breakdown sections

Figure 7.6

- Navigate to the Outro section of your song.
- Right-click on the Vocode Bass level fader and select Edit Automation from the drop-down menu.
- A new lane will appear in the mixer track, labeled Channel 1 level.
- You could use the Pencil tool to draw in an automation clip, but you've already got a clip copied to your clipboard that you can utilize here.
- Paste the clip by pressing Control + V.
- The clip will be copied to the Channel 5 level lane.
- Now, drag the clip up to Channel 1 at Bar 187.
- Then, extend the clip to the end of the Outro section and double-click on it to enter the Edit mode.
- Adjust the node to 55.
- Last, click on the background to exit the Edit Automation mode.

Figure 7.7

- Next, Option + Drag the Vocode Bass automation clip from the Outro section into the Breakdown section.
- Resize the clip to twenty-four bars and double-click on it to enter the Edit Automation mode.
- Adjust the first node to 50.
- Using the Pencil tool, draw two new nodes at 107. You may need to change the snap value to 32 to be able to move the nodes around.
- Next, set the first node at 50 and the second at 46.

Figure 7.8

- Now, use Option + Drag to drag the Vocode Bass automation clip from the Breakdown section to the Intro section.
- Resize the clip to thirty-two bars and then double-click on it to enter the Edit Automation mode.
- Adjust the first node to 55.
- Then, set the Snap value to the Bar setting.
- Lastly, rubber-band select around the 2 nodes at bar nine and drag them to bar 17.

Finalizing the Mix

The final task to complete for your mix is to engage the Mastering Suite.

Figure 7.9

I tend to ignore the Combinator controls and prefer make adjustments to the devices themselves.

When it comes to using effects processors, I'm a firm believer in the "less is more" philosophy, especially during the final mastering stage.

As you've spent a considerable time fine-tuning your mix, you will not have to spend a lot of time correcting mistakes. Instead, you will be able to focus on sweetening the mix with subtle EQ and stereo enhancement, while the compressor will enable you to glue the mix together. The Maximizer is especially effective in that it will allow you to get your mix as loud as possible without causing clipping to occur.

EQ

You will only require minimal use of the EQ, as the track is already well balanced.
- Engage the 30 Hz low-cut filter setting.
- Bypass the High- and Low-Shelf EQs.
- Set Parametric 1 to a subtle boost of 0.06 dB, at 57 Hz.
- Last, set Parametric 2 to a subtle boost of 0.03 dB, at 659 Hz.

Stereo Imager

When utilizing the Imager, it is useful to engage the solo functions located along the right side. These allow you to monitor the two bands and adjust the width of the stereo field. Again, a stereo mix like this won't require too much adjusting. Typically, the higher content is best spread wide, while the low frequencies should be left narrow.

- First, set the Hi Band to Solo and the XOver Frequency to 413.
- Adjust the widening to 13.
- Then solo the Lo Band and adjust the width to –9.

Compressor

A compressor, when used properly, can really help the tracks of your song to gel together appropriately. In this case, you won't need a lot of compression, as you want to keep the dynamic range intact.

- First, set the Input Gain to 3.8 dB.
- Then, adjust the Threshold setting to –23.5 and the Ratio to 2.87:1.
- Now, set the Attack to 70 ms, to allow plenty of the original transients to come through in the mix.

The Release needs to be relatively fast, with a setting of 171 ms to allow the compressor to reset itself.

The Output Gain will be increased to 0.04 dB.

Maximizer

This is the most extreme effect you will be using for your mix. It is intended to sufficiently pump up the volume level without clipping or stifling the mix.

- Set the Input Gain to 3.9.
- The Limiter should be engaged with the 4 ms Look Ahead button turned on. This allows for a four-second lead time, which ensures that nothing can slip by and clip your Hardware Interface.
- Notice that the Attack is slow while the Release is fast, not unlike our compressor.
- The Output Gain should be set at 4.1.
- You will also be utilizing the Soft Clip feature, which smoothes out any spikes with a pleasant-sounding harmonic distortion. This will result in a desirable softening to the overall effect.

At this point, you are ready to mix this track down to a stereo .wav or .aiff file. In the next chapter, you'll explore setting up and using Reason for live performance.

Chapter 8

PERFORMING LIVE WITH REASON

The ability to perform live using Reason became a reality with the advent of the Combinator. Reason has always had the capability of enabling the use of multiple controllers to play a variety of instruments in real time, simultaneously.

Figure 8.1

With the Combinator and the new Dr. OctoRex, it is now possible to load up several sections of a song and have them trigger, via MIDI, notes in unison.

Fig. 8.1 shows a basic setup that I have created to be used for the live playback of backing tracks.

In the rack you will find six Dr. OctoRexes loaded with loops. Each Dr. OctoRex has the same loop loaded into various slots. This is so that you can create a basic song structure that can then be triggered by selecting keys E0 to B0 as designated to a MIDI controller.

Selecting E0 will cause Loop Slot 1 to trigger in each of the six Dr. OctoRexes. Notice how some slots are left intentionally blank to create a build, which is accomplished by adding new elements as you play higher notes on the scale.

In the arrangement window you will find the Combinator track, which controls all six Dr. OctoRexes, as well as each individual Dr. Octorex. This enables greater flexibility in triggering individual loops on the fly.

Another benefit that Reason offers is the ability to lock a controller to a specific device. The master keyboard will always follow the selection displayed in the arrangement window, so it's possible to set up multiple controllers to control several different facets of a live setup.

Let's take a look at how to build a live rack and lock a controller to a designated device.

Building a Live Set Rack

- With a new session open, create a Combinator.
- Make sure the Device Window is showing and selected. This is indicated by a red bar across the top of the section.
- Create a 14:2 mixer.
- Select the mixer inside the Combinator and create three Dr. OctoRex Loop Players.
- For the first Dr. OctoRex, load Beyer & Lekebusch / Bottom Loops from the Dr. OctoRex Patches > Drums > Electronic Drums > –Beyer Lekebusch folder.
- Then, for the second Dr. OctoRex, load Beyer & Lekebusch / Top Loops –1 from the Dr. OctoRex Patches > Drums > Electronic Drums > –Beyer Lekebusch folder.
- And then, for the third Dr. OctoRex, load Percussion / Tabla 75–2 from the Dr. OctoRex Patches > Percussion folder.
- Next, navigate to the C0 octave of your keyboard controller, which is three octaves down from middle C.
- Press E0 on your controller.
- All three Dr. OctoRex Loop Players will start playing Slot 1 in unison.
- Press F0 and all three of the Dr. OctoRex Loop Players will play Slot 2 in unison. The same procedure can be repeated for any key from E0 to B0.

Locking a Controller to a Device

If you have more than one controller available, with Reason it's possible to lock a device to a specific instrument, or another device.

First, confirm that Reason recognizes your controller, via Preferences > Keyboards and Control Surfaces.

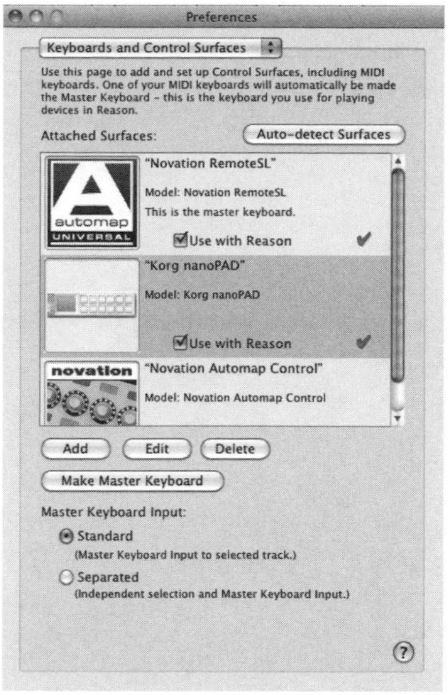

Figure 8.2

If your controller isn't displayed, try activating the Auto-detect Surfaces button. You also have the option to add a controller manually or use one of the generic model settings listed in the Other menu option.

In this example, I've added a Korg nanoPAD. Note that a Novation Remote controller has also been assigned

Once Reason recognizes your controller, you can lock a device to it.

Options > Surface Locking

Select Surface Locking from the Options menu.

Under Surface, select the controller to be locked. In this case, you will be selecting the Korg nanoPAD.

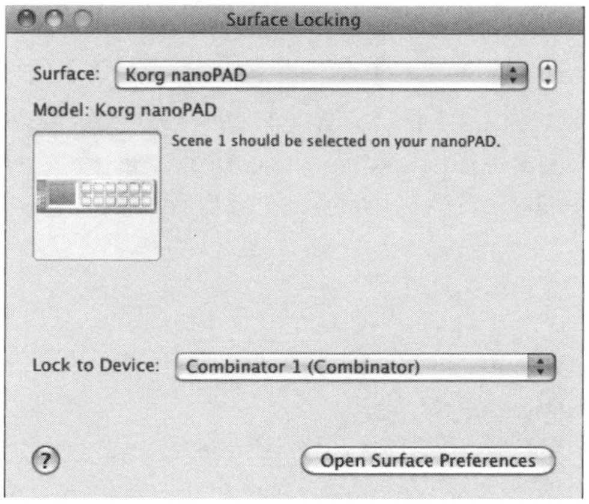

Figure 8.3

Under Lock to Device, select the Combinator.

Now, when you navigate to a different device, your nanoPAD will always be available to trigger the Combinator, including all three Dr. OctoRexes, in unison.

Edit Menu > Surface Lock Device

The Edit menu can be used to choose a controller and select the device to which to lock it. In this case, selecting Edit > Lock Korg nanoPAD to this device would be the correct setting. An even easier way to make this selection is to right-click on the device and select the Lock nanoPAD setting.

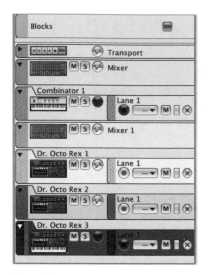

Figure 8.4

Another great way to introduce additional variation into a mix is to create tracks for each device within your Combinator. Fig. 8.4 displays three Dr. OctoRex Loop Players and the mixer. As the Novation controller is set up to be your master controller, you are able select any of these tracks and have control over the device that is independent of the nanoPAD control over the Combinator.

Remote Override

Many controllers come complete with ready-made templates for user-friendly, plug-and-play control over Reason. These templates usually consist of a logical layout of controls for each available device, in addition to a full breadth of control of every parameter.

However, you may find that when working on a set for live performance, these logically designed templates won't provide you with an easy way to control parameters. If you find yourself constantly juggling between tracks, its useful to know that there is an easier way.

Edit Remote Override

Selecting Edit Remote Override from the Options menu enables you to remap any parameter of any device to any available physical controller.

When you first engage Edit Remote Override, you will see that all the devices in the rack are grayed out. When you select a device, you'll see either blue arrows or yellow circles, depending on which track has been selected by your Master Keyboard input.

The blue arrows (see Fig. 8.5) denote all the available parameters that can be remapped.

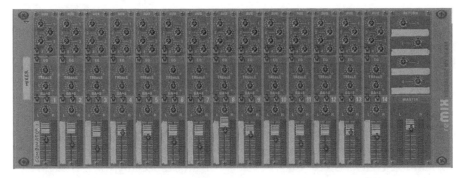

Figure 8.5

In Fig. 8.6, you see the same mixer with the Master Keyboard input selected on the designated track. Notice, now, how the previously displayed blue arrows have been replaced with yellow circles. This is to distinguish them from the parameters that have already been routed to the controller.

Figure 8.6

It's important to bear in mind, when approaching the Remote Override, that any parameter you assign will take precedent over preexisting or previously routed parameters.

For instance, if you were to remote override Channel 1's fader assignment, then any device that would normally use the fader designated to your controller would lose its control.

It's definitely a tradeoff, because once you commit to overriding some parameters, you will lose a bit of functionality. However, for use in a live set, this is a positive attribute, because such ability gives you total customization over your set.

Having multiple controllers provides excellent benefits, especially when you can lock controllers, override parameters, and command full control using your master keyboard input. It is even possible to have multiple controllers mapped to the same parameter.

Programming Remote Overrides

To create an assignment, enable Edit Remote Override from the Options menu.

Next, select the device you wish to override.

Then double-click on the parameter you wish to override.

A yellow spinning lighting bolt will appear on the screen. Move the controller's fader, knob, or button to assign this to a location. Once assigned, the parameter will maintain a static lightning bolt hovering above it.

Figure 8.7

Another way to assign a controller is to right-click on a parameter and select Edit Remote Override Mapping.

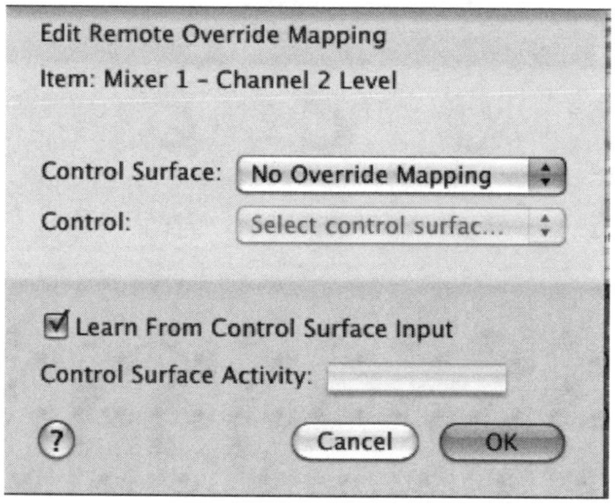

Figure 8.8

Next, a text box will open, enabling you to either manually assign the Control Surface and Control or use the Learn from Control Surface Input.

Incidentally, you do not have to be in Remote Edit Override Mode to remap a control. You can also do so from the standard view by right-clicking on a parameter and selecting Edit Remote Override Mapping.

In Fig 8.9, note how Filter Freq and Filter Res have been routed to Rotary 1 and then mapped to Fader 4. The ability to control multiple parameters via the programmer on the Combinator and to then map these controls to a tactile knob or slider, really adds a new dimension to the live setup.

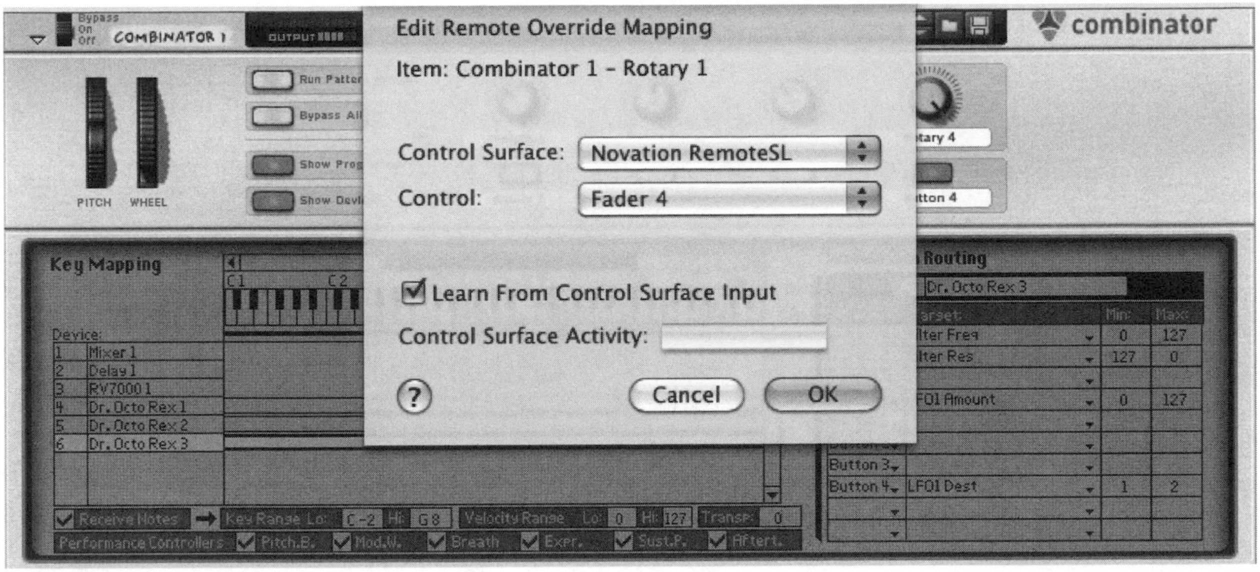

Figure 8.9

Keyboard Control

Another useful function for assigning control is the Enable Keyboard Remote, also found on the Option menu.

This function permits the assignment of control to the computer keyboard.

Certain keys are blocked because they are already hardwired as key commands; for example, Q–U for tool selection, or the numeric pad for transport controls.

Most keys can be accessed with the use of Shift as a modifier.

Figure 8.10

Keyboard Control Edit Mode

To make assignments, you can enter this mode with the Enable Keyboard Remote function turned on.

When selecting a device, note how all the assignable controls are denoted with a gold arrow. Double-clicking on an arrow causes a gold spinning square to appear.

Once a selection is made, a static gold box appears with the newly labeled keystroke.

Note that the value for the control is the minimum and maximum. For instance, assigning a keystroke to a channel fader will cause the value to switch between 0 and 127.

Although this can limit the functionality, it is especially useful for switches and buttons. If assigned to a button with multiple options, such as LFO waveform, the control will cycle through the available options.

Additional Overrides

Another useful option for controlling different aspects of Reason is its Additional Overrides, which enable you to control Reason from you MIDI controller. Many of these overrides would not be possible from standard key commands.

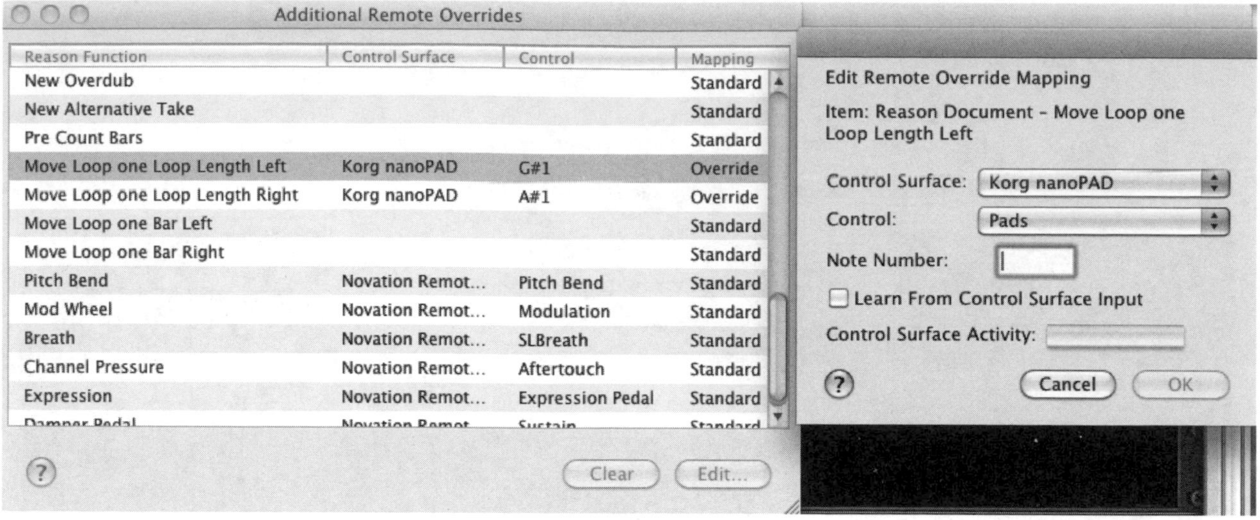

Figure 8.11

In Fig. 8.11, you will see how to assign Move Loop One Loop Length Left to a pad on the Korg nanoKONTROL.

By pressing G#1 and A#1, you are able to move the L and R locators by a predefined value. This is a fantastic way to loop sections of the Reason sequencer on the fly, using your controller.

DJing with Reason

Performing a DJ style set is completely possible using Reason, as it is easy to have multiple songs open and running simultaneously. Although there is no method to sync two songs together without utilizing two separate computers, if you are a solo performer using one computer, you can use the number 1 on the numeric pad to repeatedly restart from the left locator. This function is very similar to the Tap Tempo button found on the transport. It takes a little practice, but once you get the hang of it, you can manually synchronize two songs as long as the tempos match appropriately. To do this effectively, you will want to have a proper sound card with at least two stereo outputs, to provide the cue necessary to achieving successful transitions.

In the next chapter, you will explore ReWire and how to use Reason as a sound module within other programs.

Chapter 9
ReWire

R eWire is a technology that lets Reason be used as a sound module from within a third-party digital audio workstation.

Some of the benefits of using ReWire include the ability to utilize third-party plug-ins and effects, to connect with hardware synthesizers, and to record audio.

Before ReWire, if you had wanted to synchronize two applications, you would be forced to use the IAC (inter-application connection), which offered only MIDI functionality in a tedious and clunky process.

With ReWire 2, you are now able to stream up to 256 audio tracks from Reason and over 4,000 MIDI tracks into Reason. Plus, you have the extra benefit of having the name of every Reason device show up in your host program. This makes it an especially elegant method for combining the power of Reason with other programs such as ProTools, Logic Pro, Cubase, Digital Performer, and Ableton Live both to record audio parts and use outboard synthesizers.

Setting Up ReWire

You have two data streams when working with ReWire. The audio stream is routed from Reason to the host application. The MIDI stream routes MIDI from the host to Reason. At the very least, the audio stream must be set up.

Audio ReWire

The setup process is pretty painless, as most functions are handled automatically.

We'll be using Logic Pro to demonstrate the process. There are resources available online from Propellerhead, too.

You must first launch Logic before Reason. Launching Reason first will cause the two applications to be open without ReWire, but not to worry, as this will not damage anything on your system.

With Logic open, launch Reason.

Figure 9.1

Figure 9.2

The first thing to notice when Reason is launched is that the Hardware Interface unusually displays your audio driver, which now registers ReWire Slave Mode. This is to indicate that ReWire has been activated.

If you are planning on rewiring a completed Reason project, you will need to decide whether you'll be using the mixer in Reason and outputting a stereo mix, or setting each instrument to its own channel within the host application. Either way, the process is essentially the same.

Figure 9.3

Because you will be building a session from scratch to observe how to use Reason effectively as a sound module, you will first need to add some instruments.

Start by creating a Thor, a Subtractor, and then a ReDrum.

Press Tab to display the rear of the rack and cable the instruments to the audio output section of the Hardware Interface. The Thor is connected to Channels 1 and 2, the Subtractor is connected to Channel 3, and the ReDrum is connected to Channels 5 and 6.

If you hit Play on either transport, both programs will start to play in sync. Note that the L and R locators are both locked as well.

In Logic, you'll need to create three Aux tracks for the instruments connected to the Hardware Interface and assign the input to the used Hardware Interface channels.

Figure 9.4

In Fig. 9.4, you see three Aux tracks, each with input set to the proper channels. Notice that I've programmed a simple kick pattern to the ReDrum, as indicated by the resulting audio displayed on Aux 3 in Logics mixer.

If you were using Reason's sequencer to trigger the instruments from a song created in Reason, then you are now ready to add additional instruments and effects to your production.

MIDI ReWire

If you are planning on triggering the Reason Instruments from within Logic, you will first need to set up the ReWire MIDI tracks.

With most audio applications, simply creating a MIDI track and assigning its output to the proper Reason instrument is pretty straightforward.

Logic is an object-based program and therefore needs to have the proper objects created within its environment, to access this functionality.

To execute this, first open Logic's environment from the Windows menu.

By default, Logic opens to the Mixer layer in the environment. It doesn't matter where you place the ReWire objects, just as long as they exist within the environment. Then, from the New menu, select Internal > ReWire.

Figure 9.5

The newly created object will appear in the Environment window.

With the ReWire object selected, turn your attention to the parameter box in the upper left corner of the Environment window.

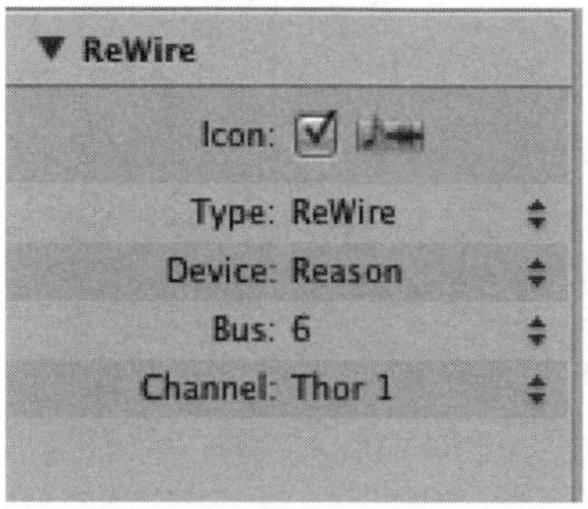

Figure 9.6

Now, confirm the following settings have been made.

Type
Type should be set to ReWire.

Device
Any ReWire-capable devices will appear in this drop-down window. Ensure that this is set to Reason.

Bus
The default setting of 6 is the correct setting for Reason Instruments.

Channel
- Click on the channel drop-down menu and select the Thor from the available list.
- Next, use the option-click method to create two more copies of the ReWire object.
- Change the channel settings for these ReWire objects to reflect the remaining instruments in your Reason rack.
- Last, close the Environment window.
- Now, from Logic's arrangement page, create a new track by double-clicking in the blank area just below the track listed as Aux 3.
- A new track entitled Aux 4 will be created.
- Right-click on the track name and navigate to Reassign Track > Mixer > ReWire.
- Now, assign the newly created ReWire track a more descriptive name by doubling-clicking on it and typing "Thor."

- With the ReWire track Thor selected, double-click again to create a new track. Because the current track is also a ReWire track, Logic will create a new track of the same type of track listed in ascending order.

Follow this process to create one more track and rename it to reflect the channel assignment.

You now have a total of six tracks in the arrangement window: three for the ReWire MIDI and three for the ReWire audio.

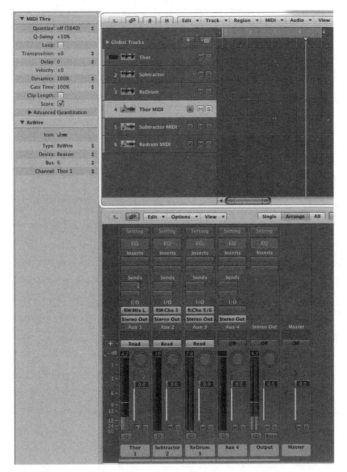

Figure 9.7

Now, selecting a ReWire MIDI track and playing a MIDI controller will send the MIDI signal to the instrument in the Reason rack. The output of the Reason instrument is routed to its respective designated audio track.

The last thing you'll need to set is the ReWire behavior found in the Logic audio preferences. To do this, change from Playback to Record.

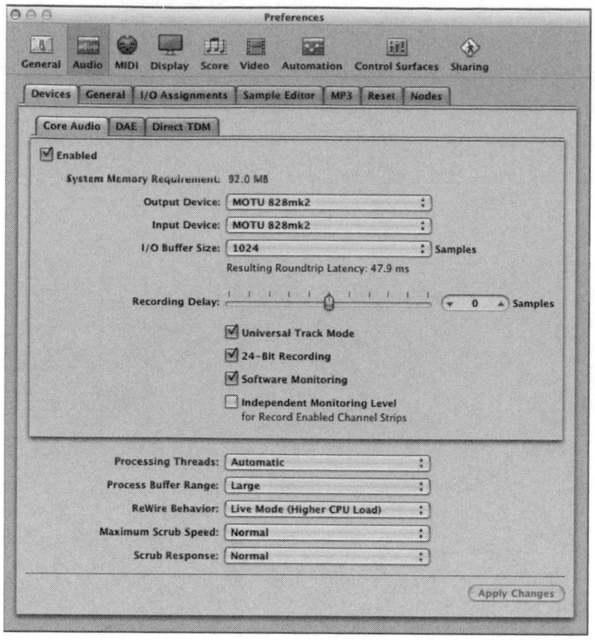
Preferences
General
Audio
MIDI
Display
Score
Video
Automation
Control Surfaces
Sharing
Devices
General
I/O Assignments
Sample Editor
MP3
Reset
Nodes
Core Audio
DAE
Direct TDM
Enabled
System Memory Requirement: 92.0 MB
Output Device: MOTU 828mk2
Input Device: MOTU 828mk2
I/O Buffer Size: 1024 Samples
Resulting Roundtrip Latency: 47.9 ms
Recording Delay: 0 Samples
Universal Track Mode
24-Bit Recording
Software Monitoring
Independent Monitoring Level
for Record Enabled Channel Strips
Processing Threads: Automatic
Process Buffer Range: Large
ReWire Behavior: Live Mode (Higher CPU Load)
Maximum Scrub Speed: Normal
Scrub Response: Normal
Apply Changes

Figure 9.8

Chapter 10
REASON AND RECORD

In 2009, Propellerhead released Record, an audio-recording platform that takes much of the same design, layout, and function from its predecessor Reason. In comparison, Record is geared toward musicians and live band recording. It also features simple, intuitive controls that allow the music-making process to occur organically and, more important, without the technology getting in the way.

The software offers a mixing console based on the Solid State Logic 9000K and, as such, the sound quality and functionality is nothing short of breathtaking.

But Record, itself, also ships with an ID8 instrument, guitar, and bass amp simulators from Line 6, as well as MClass effects and some other impressive selections. The software is aimed toward live musicians; however, if you own Reason, integration into Record is automatic, providing every aspect of Reason plus a whole lot more. I, personally, am a huge fan of the Reason/Record combo, because no matter what style of music you make, it's well worth the investment for all that it offers.

ReWire features great functionality, although it's still missing some core integration between certain software platforms. If you are looking for a DAW to record audio and work with Reason, then this could be the best match for you. Think of it as Reason, but on steroids!

I could easily write an entire book on Record, but in the last chapter of this book on Reason Advanced, I will guide you through just the basics, to give you the foundation you need to get up and running with this versatile and easy-to-use software.

The Record Interface

Record is broken up into three sections: the sequencer, rack, and mixer.

The Sequencer

The sequencer looks and behaves exactly like the sequencer in Reason.

Figure 10.1

Notice the exact same track column, tool sets, and transport controls, as well as the overview of instruments located on the right side of the display. The blue-outlined box allows for quick navigation of tracks within the sequencer window. Simply click or grab, and the window snaps to the intended view automatically.

The Rack

Notice how the rack is double width, which really helps with organization.

Figure 10.2

All instruments and the effects are housed within the rack. There's an overview section on the right side, which allows for quick navigation over the entire rack.

Figure 10.3

In Fig. 10.3, you will find two new types of devices displayed in the rack. The first is the Audio Track device and the second is the Mix Channel device.

These devices serve to interconnect the sequencer, rack, and mixer. For every audio track in your sequencer window, there will be a dedicated Audio Track device, which also connects with the Mix Channel strip.

On the Mix Channel device, notice how Show Programmer and Insert FX are folded into view, and that their functionality resembles the Combinator in design. There are the familiar four rotary controls and four buttons on the left, and modulation routing is located on the right.

Instruments can even be loaded into the Insert section to take further advantage of the full range of modulation routing and controls.

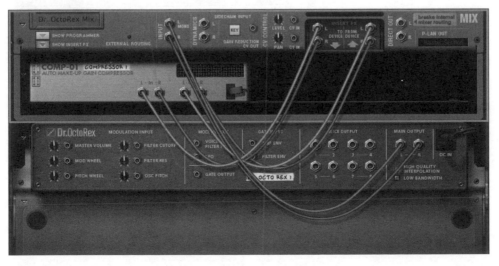

Figure 10.4

The rear of the rack, accessible by pressing the Tab button, reveals the connection between the Dr. OctoRex Loop Player and the Mix Channel interface, with the Comp 01 being connected via the insert Send and Return connections.

The Mixer

The mixer, which is modeled after the SSL9000K, features an incredible amount of control, and for some, this may be somewhat off-putting.

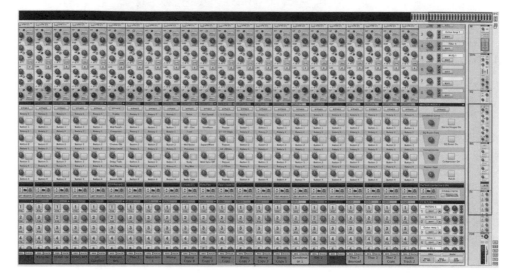

Figure 10.5

Whatever you think at first; do not let it intimidate you. Its purpose that of the 14:2 mixer, albeit with many more bells and whistles, but essentially it is the same. Let's take a closer look and break down what is displayed, so you will better understand how it functions.

Input

The Input section offers control over gain and the signal path of the dynamics, the EQ, and the Insert section.

Input Gain

The Input Gain controls the input of the signal coming in from either an audio input on the Hardware Interface or from a designated instrument.

Signal Path

The dedicated buttons of the Signal Path section allow you to change the signal flow. The default has the signal running through the dynamics, EQ, and inserts. These buttons switch the order to offer various combinations.

Figure 10.6

Dynamics

The Dynamics section offers a dedicated compressor and a gate with key input to enable side chain effects.

Figure 10.7

Compressor

The compressor offers the standard controls: Ratio, Threshold, and Release. The Peak button switches the compressor from an average setting to a peak setting; the Fast button changes the compressor's attack.

Gate

The gate controls include Range, Threshold, Release, and Hold. It may also be switched to Expander mode via the EXP button.

EQ

High- and Low-Shelf Filters

The HF and LF (red and black) sections of the EQ are shelf filters. The Bell button switches from shelf to bell curve.

HMF

The High-Mid Frequency section is a fully parametric equalizer with Frequency, Gain, and Q controls.

LMF

The Low-Mid Frequency section is also a fully functioning parametric equalizer with the same controls as the HMF, only it operates at a lower frequency range.

Figure 10.8

Figure 10.9

Insert

The Insert section offers the same controls as the Mix and Audio devices found in the rack.

At the bottom of the section are the Browse and Save Effects buttons. Pressing the Browse Patch button allows you to peruse a multitude of great-sounding preset effects, way beyond what Reason offers.

Insert FX Controls

There are four programmable knobs and buttons, and multiple parameters may be gathered together and set to a single knob or button.

FX Sends

The FX Sends section offers eight sends with level controls and dedicated pre buttons to switch any send to prefader mode.

Fader

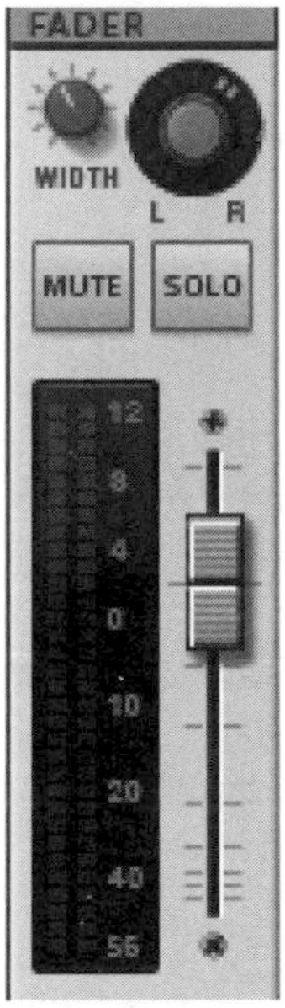

The Fader section offers the usual controls with a level fader, and Solo and Mute buttons.

Pan

The Pan control offers a width control that goes way beyond simple left and right. The width allows you to dial in and place your sound with precision and control within the stereo field.

Master Section

The Master section is the heart and soul of any console. It offers extensive control over the FX send and return, master inserts, master fader level control, monitor control, and the famous SSL Stereo Bus compressor.

Master Compressor

The master compressor is faithfully modeled after the much-sought-after SSL Stereo Bus compressor. It provides the sonic glue that brings your tracks together and gives them a professional and polished sheen. It features the standard compression controls, with a key input and VU meter settings.

FX Send

Dedicated FX Send controls allow you to control the levels going to an effects device.

This is incredibly helpful when sending multiple sends to an effect, because it gives you the ability to lower the Gain stage before the effects without changing the overall balance of the sends.

Figure 10.10

Figure 10.11

Figure 10.12

Figure 10.13

Master Insert

The Master Insert section offers the same control as the Channel Insert section, with similar dedicated control knobs and buttons. A wide variety of master effects patches are also included.

Figure 10.14

FX Return

The FX Return section offers level and pan control over sound coming from any effect.

Figure 10.15

Master Fader

The master fader offers level control over the entire mix. In addition, it adds a Level knob for the control room output and enables independent monitoring of each FX send and return.

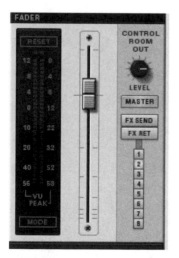

Figure 10.16

In Conclusion

As you can see, the Reason/Record combo offers a comprehensive set of tools for creating and mixing with the most professional of results. If you like working with Reason, then you're going to really love working with Record!

APPENDIX: THE DVD-ROM

On the enclosed DVD-Rom, I have included twelve instructional videos to help you delve deeper into sound design and mixing. In addition, I've also included three Reason song files to be used with chapters 6 and 7.

Video Tutorials

The following tutorials are designed to help clarify and cement certain topics throughout the book.

1. Synthesis Overview

This video covers the basic operation of an analog subtractive synthesizer.

Figure A.1

2. Subtractor

Using the concepts discussed in the Synthesis Overview video, you'll examine the Subtractor Analog Synthesizer.

Figure A.2

3. Thor

This is a two-part video tutorial covering the Thor Polysonic Synthesizer. The first part covers the Synth controls; the second, the routing matrix and step sequencer.

Figure A.3

4. Malstrom

This video explains the operation and use of the Malstrom Graintable Synthesizer.

Figure A.4

5. Sampling with the NN-19

This video tutorial covers the concept of sampling with examples from the NN-19
Digital Sampler.

Figure A.5

6. NN-XT

The NN-XT video tutorial explains advanced sampling techniques.

Figure A.6

7. Dr. OctoRex Loop Player

This video covers the use and operation of the Dr. OctoRex Loop Player.

Figure A.7

8. ReDrum Drum Computer

This video covers the operation of the ReDrum Drum computer.

Figure A.8

9. Kong Drum Designer

This video tutorial explores the operation of the Kong Drum Designer.

Figure A.9

10. BV512 Digital Vocoder

This video shows the setup and use of the BV512 Digital Vocoder.

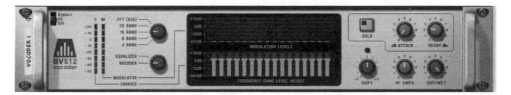

Figure A.10

11. Arranging and Mixing

This video describes what is covered in chapters 6 and 7, including the use of the three Reason song files contained on this DVD.

Figure A.11

12. Record Overview

This video is an overview of Propellerhead's Record software. Topics covered are the new rack interface and the new mixer modeled after the SSL9000K mixing console.

Figure A.12

Reason Song Files

The following three song files are to be used in conjunction with their respective chapters.

Under the Gun: Chapter 6—Advanced Sequencing.rns

This song file is to be used with chapter 6 in the book. Please load this song when beginning chapter 6

Under the Gun: Chapter 7—Advanced Mixing (Start).rns

This song file is to be used with chapter 7 in the book. It's also the finished version of chapter 6 and can be used to check your work.

Under the Gun: Chapter 7—Advanced Mixing (Finished). rns

This song file is the final version of the song "Under the Gun," with all its mixing, automation, and mastering effects applied.

Under the Gun.mp3

This is an MP3 file bounced down from the Under the Gun---Final Mix.rns song file.

INDEX